"Completely compelling . . . For all the sadness and dysfunction in Guirgis's plays, he nevertheless seems to extend hope— to his characters in their v~ nce in theirs. You could cry (ply to laugh instead."

RK

"Guirgis, like other storytellers who explore the sacred and the profane, is most interested in how grace transforms us. His empathetic, poetic tales of ex-cons, addicts, and other men whom society would label losers return us, again and again, to a world that Guirgis, by virtue of his particular religion—the church of the streets—illuminates with the bright and crooked light of his faith."

—HILTON ALS, NEW YORKER

"This is a black comedy, and the dialogue snaps and crackles . . . Particularly funny—but also unexpectedly tender."

—ELISABETH VINCENTELLI, NEW YORK POST

"Quite possibly his most accomplished piece to date . . . Like all of Guirgis's work, Riverside is populated with salty, blue-collar New Yorkers with a penchant for trouble . . . [but] some moments are so quietly observant you almost feel as if you're eavesdropping."

—JASON CLARK, ENTERTAINMENT WEEKLY

"Explores, with both street-smart, sometimes-profane wit and disarming tenderness, the different ways in which we cling to, reject and exploit faith. Never one to settle for simple answers or snarky observations, Guirgis portrays his characters, and their twisting journeys, with humor and compassion . . . To survive the imperfect world these folks inhabit—and try to attain grace in— is something of a miracle in itself, and Guirgis, in his predictably unsentimental way, finds warmth and wonder in their struggle."

—ELYSA GARDNER, USA TODAY

"A vivid group portrait . . . Like life, [this play] switches from tender to gritty to shocking."

—JOE DZIEMIANOWICZ, *NEW YORK DAILY NEWS*

"Absorbing and highly entertaining . . . Which current American playwright creates conversation as wonderfully loopy as that of Guirgis? I've been in love with his work for fifteen years."

—BRENDAN LEMON, *FINANCIAL TIMES*

"A nuanced, beautifully written play about a retired police officer faced with eviction that uses dark comedy to confront questions of life and death."

—PULITZER PRIZE CITATION

"A hard-headed kitchen-sink comedy, one that has serious things to say about lower-middle-class urban life, race relations and the corrosive effects of resentment on the human soul. Yet the playwright makes his points in an unfailingly unpredictable way . . . Mr. Guirgis has a firm grasp of the endless complexity of human motivation."

—TERRY TEACHOUT, *WALL STREET JOURNAL*

"Hilariously pungent and deceptively complex, the play feels fully, deeply lived-in . . . Pops is an endlessly fascinating figure, capable of both casual viciousness and tender solicitude."
—Frank Scheck, *Hollywood Reporter*

"Gripping . . . This dazzling display of decadence and depression is written with the alarming impact of being run down by a wayward sanitation truck . . . *Between Riverside and Crazy* is the kind of rich, dynamic theater you almost never see anymore—fresh, savage, original, two-fisted and relevant."

—REX REED, *NEW YORK OBSERVER*

BETWEEN RIVERSIDE *and* CRAZY

BETWEEN RIVERSIDE *and* CRAZY

Stephen Adly Guirgis

THEATRE COMMUNICATIONS GROUP   NEW YORK   2015

Between Riverside and Crazy is copyright © 2015 by Stephen Adly Guirgis

Between Riverside and Crazy is published by Theatre Communications Group, Inc., 520 Eighth Avenue, 24th Floor, New York, NY 10018

All rights reserved. Except for brief passages quoted in newspaper, magazine, radio or television reviews, no part of this book may be reproduced in any form or by any means, electronic or mechanical, including photocopying or record-ing, or by an information storage and retrieval system, without permission in writing from the publisher. Professionals and amateurs are hereby warned that this material, being fully protected under the Copyright Laws of the United States of America and all other countries of the Berne and Universal Copyright Conventions, is subject to a royalty. All rights, including but not limited to, professional, amateur, recording, motion picture, recitation, lecturing, public reading, radio and television broadcasting, and the rights of translation into foreign languages are expressly reserved. Particular emphasis is placed on the question of readings and all uses of this book by educational institutions, per-mission for which must be secured from the author's representative: John Buz-zetti, William Morris Endeavor, 1325 Avenue of the Americas, New York, NY 10019, (212) 586-5100.

The publication of *Between Riverside and Crazy* by Stephen Adly Guirgis, through TCG's Book Program, is made possible in part by the New York State Council on the Arts with the support of Governor Andrew Cuomo and the New York State Legislature.

TCG books are exclusively distributed to the book trade by Consortium Book Sales and Distribution.

Library of Congress Cataloging-in-Publication Data
Guirgis, Stephen Adly.
Between Riverside and crazy / Stephen Adly Guirgis.—First edition.
pages ; cm
ISBN 978-1-55936-517-8 (hardcover)
ISBN 978-1-55936-515-4 (softcover)
ISBN 978-1-55936-842-1 (ebook)
I. Title.
PS3607.U49B48   2015
812'.6—dc23   2015025584

Book design and composition by Lisa Govan
Cover art by AKA NYC Limited, courtesy of Atlantic Theater Company
Cover design by Monet Cogbill

First Edition, October 2015

BETWEEN RIVERSIDE *and* CRAZY

PRODUCTION HISTORY

Between Riverside and Crazy received its world premiere on July 31, 2014 at the Atlantic Theater Company (Neil Pepe, Artistic Director; Jeffory Lawson, Managing Director) in New York City. It was directed by Austin Pendleton; the set design was by Walt Spangler, the costume design was by Alexis Forte, the lighting design was by Keith Parham, the music and sound design were by Ryan Rumery; the production stage manager was Kelly Ice. The cast was:

WALTER "POPS" WASHINGTON	Stephen McKinley Henderson
JUNIOR	Ray Anthony Thomas
OSWALDO	Victor Almanzar
LULU	Rosal Colón
CHURCH LADY	Liza Colón-Zayas
DETECTIVE O'CONNOR	Elizabeth Canavan
LIEUTENANT CARO	Michael Rispoli

This production of *Between Riverside and Crazy* transferred to Second Stage Theatre (Carole Rothman, Artistic Director; Casey Reitz, Executive Director) in New York City on February 11, 2015. The cast and personnel remained the same with the following exceptions: the production stage manager was David Sugarman and Junior was played by Ron Cephas Jones.

CHARACTERS

WALTER "POPS" WASHINGTON
JUNIOR, his son
OSWALDO, Junior's friend
LULU, Junior's girlfriend
CHURCH LADY
DETECTIVE O'CONNOR
LIEUTENANT CARO

TIME AND PLACE

Summer, recently. Walter "Pops" Washington's pre-war apartment on Riverside Drive is a grand old railroad flat with chandeliers and a river view, but it's seen better days since the death of Pops's beloved wife just before Christmas. Once meticulously cared for, the place has devolved into a mix of beautiful fixtures, family mementos and antique furniture competing for survival with dust, stains, garbage, leaks and unattended junk. In the kitchen, the wallpaper peels. In the living room, the twin chaise longue sofas are close to surrender, the scuffed hardwood floors sport small matching piles of ancient dog shit—and by the window a long dead but still lit Christmas tree maintains a stooping, drooped vigil. Still, the place retains its dignity and charm—and the comforting aroma of decades of pot roasts and chicken dinners lets us know we're in a genuine old-school New York City family home. It's a rent-controlled Palace ruled by a grieving despot King. It's also prime Manhattan real estate that, if deregulated, would easily fetch ten times its current rent.

ACT ONE

SCENE 1

Kitchen Table. Saturday Morning.

Pops eats pie, sips whiskey and drinks tea. He sits in his deceased wife's old wheelchair. The small kitchen table is beat up, but the fork is polished silver and his plate and teacup are fine china. Pops tries very hard to ignore Oswaldo, who loudly chews almonds throughout—

OSWALDO: How's your pie? Good?

POPS: Fine.

OSWALDO: Yeah but—wanna try some of these fresh organic raw almonds from Whole Foods instead? Because my caseworker over at the place, he a real ball breaker like how I told you, but ever since I took his suggestion and switched my breakfast to almonds and health water instead of, you know—Ring Dings with bologna and Fanta Grape—

POPS: Oswaldo—

OSWALDO: See: the Ring Dings and bologna and Fanta Grape, it turns out, that's what doctors and *People* magazine call "emotional eating" on my part—on account of I only ate that shit because those foods made me feel "safe and taken care of" back when I was a kid who was never "safe or taken care of." But now, I'm a adult, right? So I don't gotta eat like that no more, and I can take care of myself by getting all fit and diesel like how I'm doing from eating these almonds and making other healthful choices like I been making. And so, I'm not trying to get all up in your business, but maybe that's also the reason you always be eating pie—because of, like, you got emotionalisms—ya know?

POPS: Emotionalisms.

OSWALDO: I know—it sounded funny at first to me too—but emotionalisms is real, and pie—don't take this wrong—but they say pie is like poison.

POPS: Pie ain't like poison, Oswaldo—pie is like pie!

OSWALDO: I know, but they said—

POPS: Oh yeah, "They said"! "They" always saying something. Then later, they'll go and say something else that's inevitably completely ass-backwards from what they originally said! Happens all the time. For example, them almonds. Don't be surprised if we learn in the future that almonds cause cancer.

OSWALDO: Nah, they're good for you—

POPS: Yeah, "they" say that now—wait a while, see what "they" gonna say then. Now grab me that Cool Whip from out the fridge—Nestor didn't finish all my Cool Whip, did he?

OSWALDO: I'll check.

POPS: Motherfucker thinks I'm here to keep him in Cool Whip.

(Lulu enters. She's wearing very little.)

LULU: Morning, Dad.

(Lulu kisses Pops's cheek, her body rubs up on him a little.)

POPS: Morning, Lulu.

LULU: Morning, Oswaldo . . . You got something on your face.

OSWALDO: What, where?

(Lulu rubs it off Oswaldo's face.)

LULU: There. It's off.

POPS: Lulu, you don't get cold, dressed like that?

LULU: Oh I'm very warm-blooded—I can't even sleep with a sheet.

POPS: How about a little robe then, something?

LULU: In the summertime?!

OSWALDO: Cool Whip's gone—

LULU: Oh, was that yours, Dad?!

(Lulu bends over the fridge exposing herself further as she searches—)

POPS: Oh good Lord, "Full moon rising!" Lulu, mind your hindquarters—please!

(Lulu retrieves some pudding.)

LULU: Butterscotch swirl! Did you say something, Dad?

POPS: Nah, never mind. You walk the dog, Oswaldo?

LULU: Oh—I can go walk him right now, Dad!

POPS: Good. Thank you. Put some pants on though.

LULU: Oh I wouldn't go out like this, Dad! You want something from the store?

POPS: Just some cookies and juice for when that damn church lady come. Why she don't get the hint nobody wants her around here?

LULU: Dad! . . . Oh, wait—Dad? I just realized I can't actually go to the store right now—when's the church lady coming?

POPS: Ah, don't worry about it. Just be home on time for supper. We having shrimps and my special veal you like.

LULU: Oh my God for real, Dad?!

POPS: Yes, now please, go walk the damn dog.

LULU: Oh—I'll walk him right now! Shrimps and veal!

(Lulu kisses Pops on the cheek, rubs up against him a little, and exits.)

POPS: . . . Oswaldo?

OSWALDO: Yeah, Dad?

POPS: Why she call me "Dad" all the time? I ain't her dad.

OSWALDO: It's like, you know, she very fond of you. Like a term of respect. You ain't my dad either, but I still call you Dad.

POPS: She ain't right that girl.

OSWALDO: She a nice girl, Dad.

POPS: She may be nice, and she look good, but I fear the girl is retarded.

OSWALDO: . . . Oh snap, hold up. This guy in the *Post*, I know him!

POPS: Let me see that . . . Umm-hmm, just what I thought!

OSWALDO: What?

POPS: Oswaldo, three mornings out of five, you start up with, "Oh I know this dude in the paper"—

OSWALDO: But I know a lot of peoples—

POPS: Yeah, but do you know any people who ain't criminals, Oswaldo?! Cuz it's never the guy who rescued the puppy that you know. Or the brother saved a baby from a burnin' building. But any motherfucker perpetrates a felony and ends up in the *New York Post*—that's always the motherfucker you know!

OSWALDO: I'm trying to meet new peoples, Dad. I joined the Facebook . . . Matchbox.com—you heard of them? From the computer?

POPS: Just don't bring none of your old compadres around here is all's I'm saying.

OSWALDO: You're right, no doubt. And, I mean—thank you—because I really appreciate you let me stay here, Dad. And I'm gonna start paying rent real soon—

POPS: You my son's friend and a guest in my home. Guests don't pay no rent.

OSWALDO: I just wanna help—

POPS: I don't need no help! Guests don't pay no rent—ya hear?! You a guest. Period.

OSWALDO: Yeah, I feel you on that, and thank you—but also, um, I mean, I been feeling something else for a while now, but not, like, revealing it? But I feel it, ya know? It's like, a feeling?

POPS: What feeling?

OSWALDO: Well. I mean truthfully: these morning times with you, in the kitchen here, just chilling, you and me, it's like most definitely my favorite part of the day.

POPS: Cuz you a morning person.

OSWALDO: Nah, but I ain't, that's the thing. Mornings and me, we don't agree—I mean historically. Even when I was locked up, they knew, don't communicate with me till after lunch. But here—I like mornings here—cuz, you know, cuz I enjoy spending time with you.

POPS: Well, me too—

OSWALDO: Yeah but see, my feeling I was referring to before—is maybe you're just being nice to me cuz you feel like you got no choice, cuz, like, you know, you a gentleman—but, maybe in reality, you wish I wasn't here because I annoy you sometimes, which is why, like, you always just refer to me as, you know, a guest, and actually, my caseworker, he think I prolly annoy you all the times—and if that's the truth, I could leave like today, for real, cuz I respect you too much, Dad, to be annoying you in this your place of residence—I ain't down with dat, you know? So I wanna know whatchu think about that, I mean—if that's okay, I wanna know if my feelings about your feelings are the actual feelings that's happening, and also whatchu think about that, like, honestly, so—like—whatchu think about that?—

POPS: Hold up! You hear that?!

OSWALDO: What?

POPS: That scratching on some tin sound! That's the fuckin' dog messin' with some takeout again!

OSWALDO: I'll go get him.

POPS: That ain't the point! The point is: Lulu, she juss said she gonna take the fuckin' dog with her, right?!

OSWALDO: Yeah?

POPS: Then the fool leaves without the dog! What kinda sense is that?!

OSWALDO: I'll go see what the dog be up to.

POPS: Nah. Fuck that dog. Let him choke on a chicken wing. I don't know what Junior was thinking bringing that little sonuvabitch here.

OSWALDO: I think it's cuz someone told him to get you a dog.

POPS: For what?

OSWALDO: Cuz I mean after your wife passed.

POPS: Shit—I ain't a child need to be occupied by no dog. Especially that dog. You ever notice the way he look at you, that dog? He a little bad-intent motherfucker is what he is.

OSWALDO: He cute though.

POPS: Oh, he think he cute—vain little motherfucker. Now, do me a favor, check the fridge, I think I got me a sticky bun back behind the Heinz ketchup there.

(Junior enters, dragging in a very large box and holding a large manila envelope.)

Well, look who the mule kicked in!

JUNIOR: This was posted on the door, from the landlord again.

POPS: Where you been at all night, Junior?

JUNIOR: I was here all night, just got in late and left early.

POPS: If you gonna be out all night, call.

JUNIOR: I wasn't out all night, Pop.

POPS: And how I'm supposed to know that if you don't call?

JUNIOR: But I wasn't out all night.

POPS: So you say.

JUNIOR: Oswaldo, did I come home last night and we played knock rummy and ordered Pay-Per-View with Lulu—or not?

OSWALDO: It's true, Dad. We ordered that Denzel movie that looks like it's good but it ain't?

POPS: Hope you left five-ninety-five plus tax on the cable box, Junior—"Pay-Per-View" don't mean I pay and you view.

JUNIOR: It's ten A.M., Pops, why you drinking?

POPS: Oswaldo wanted a drink, so I had one with him.

JUNIOR: Oswaldo's clean and sober, Pop—and why you using Mama's good china and the sterling silver—that's worth money!

POPS: Hear that, Oswaldo? He got the whole joint cased, appraised, and ready to move the moment I expire. Don-cha?!

JUNIOR: Oswaldo, I thought you was heading up to the Bronx this morning?

OSWALDO: I was yeah, but then I thought maybe I'd maybe hold off on dat awhile if dass okay?

JUNIOR: Right—so the phrase: "Easy Does It—But Do It"—that means what to you?

OSWALDO: . . . Means I should go to the Bronx and face my shit?

JUNIOR: So—go do that then—right, brother?

POPS: Yeah, yeah—never mind all that—now what's this big box you bringing into my house?

JUNIOR: Stuff.

POPS: From where?

JUNIOR: A friend.

POPS: You think I'm stupid? What kind of hot merchandise you got up inside that box today? He think I gone senile, Oswaldo.

JUNIOR: How many drinks you had this morning, Pops? How many he had, Oswaldo?

POPS: Just go walk that damn dog, Junior, okay?! Your girl was supposed to walk him, but then, air entered the space between her ears and she forgot. How long she staying here anyway?

JUNIOR: She's my girl, Pop, she'll stay as long as she want to.

POPS: Oswaldo say she retarded—

OSWALDO: I didn't—

POPS: What she do for a living anyway?

JUNIOR: She a student, Pop.

POPS: Oh c'mon now: I walked the beat for thirty years, Son—

JUNIOR: She go to City College, Pop! She studies!

POPS: Studies what?

JUNIOR: Accounting.

POPS: Accounting?

JUNIOR: Dass right!

POPS: Son: that girl, she a nice girl, but she don't study no accounting. Her lips move when she read the horoscope—that ain't the mark of a future accountant!

JUNIOR: Pop—

POPS: I ain't saying don't be with the girl, she a nice enough girl, but teach her a trade. She don't know how to do nothin' but walk around with her booty all out—

JUNIOR: Hey now, look at the time, I gotta go.

POPS: Go? But you just got here.

JUNIOR: Yeah, and you ain't stopped harassing me.

POPS: "Harassing"?! That what you call conversation these days?

JUNIOR: We could talk later.

POPS: How we gonna talk later with you leaving to Baltimore for the weekend?

JUNIOR: I'm not going to Baltimore. I'm canceling. And I'm fine with not going, okay?—

POPS: You hear that, Oswaldo? Hypertension run in our family—and he been hyper-tensing like a motherfucker from the moment he moved back here—and now he tryin' to front like he Superman and don't need no weekend getaway in Baltimore when clearly what he need is a damn Baltimore weekend getaway!

JUNIOR: If I go to Baltimore, you just gonna give me shit about something happened here and I wasn't here cuz I was in Baltimore. And how am I supposed to feel comfortable going anywhere anyway with you drinking all day, climbing on ladders, doing all type of recklessness—

POPS: Hey! I spent good goddamn cash money so you could catch a little breather away from me, eat yourself a soft shell crab, and go see damn Earth, Wind & Fuckin' Fire—so here's how it's going down: Audrey and her fiancé coming over for dinner 'round eight—

JUNIOR: Audrey's coming here?!

POPS: Dass right. So wear a clean shirt, be sociable and then excuse yourself promptly after dessert—and be goddamn sure that you're on that 11:55 Greyhound so you can take yourself a nice break and get your damn mind right! You hearin' me?!

OSWALDO: Don't worry, bro—me and Lulu will watch him close.

JUNIOR: Okay, Pop. Fine. But could you please do me one favor in return now and please take Mom's ol' wheelchair out the kitchen like you said you would back in January?

POPS: It's comfortable seating. Oh and by the way, I had a very nice talk with your ex-wife this morning.

JUNIOR: You did what?!—

POPS: Told her how you was enrolled in the City College now—

JUNIOR: Please don't tell Yolanda my business, Pop.

POPS: She ain't remarried yet is all I'm saying.

JUNIOR: And I pray that changes soon! Now whatchu want me to do with this envelope from the landlord?

POPS: Let the dog clean his ass with it! I'm a ex-cop, war veteran, senior citizen with a legal rent-control lease from 1978 and I never pay late—I wish they would try to fuck with me.

JUNIOR: Alright then, I'm out—

POPS: Hey—drop off my check to Lubenthal and Lubenthal on your way, it's on my dresser . . . . What?!

JUNIOR: I didn't say nothing—you hear me say something?!

POPS: Yeah but you thinking something—with that little angry prune head "pee-pee poo-poo" face like how you do.

JUNIOR: Look man, if you wanna keep paying them Lubenthal and Lubenthal shyster lawyers—even when everybody knows you shoulda settled no-fault with the city years ago—that's your business, not mine.

POPS: Number one: you don't know shit. Number two: if you had any integrity, you'd know that an honorable man can't be bought off—an honorable man doesn't just settle a lawsuit "no-fault" and lend his silence to hypocrisy and racism and the grievous violation of all our civil rights.

JUNIOR: Yeah, that's a nice story, but the fact is that if you had settled your case back when you were supposed to, then at least Mom coulda had a private nurse in her last days—

POPS: Your mother had me, she didn't need no nurse—

JUNIOR: When you got shot, Pop—you had a private nurse, didn't you?!

POPS: When I got shot, your mother needed help with me—help you were unavailable to provide from your various jail cells at Rikers and Attica, okay?!

JUNIOR: Lubenthal and Lubenthal is a fuckin' joke, Pop—they taking your money for nothing and they ain't doing shit!

POPS: Whatchu know about Lubenthal and Lubenthal? We wouldn't still have this apartment if it weren't for Lubenthal and Lubenthal! Your mother worked for Lubenthal and Lubenthal for thirty-eight years! Uncle Fred got himself a cottage, a boat, and a piece of a fine race horse down there in Montgomery—all on account of the efforts of Lubenthal and Lubenthal!

JUNIOR: Yeah, and that was when—1983? Shit—some of the best young black attorneys in this city weren't even born then—and any one of them could do you far better with the city then them ancient crooked dinosaurs Lubenthal and Lubenthal! How old is Mo Lubenthal now anyway—ninety?

POPS: Old Mo's still spry—he ain't lost a thing.

JUNIOR: Yeah, except for your money! Mom told me all about it: how you was always overly impressed and kissing that Lubenthal ass because you such an ignorant Old Head you think the only good lawyers gotta be Jews.

POPS: Your mother never said that—

JUNIOR: Oh yes she did. And that ain't all she said. Moms told me everything. About everything. So if you really wanna go all into it, I'll go in. Just say the word!

(Pause.)

Yeah, I didn't think so.

(Pause. Pops sips, grows glassy-eyed.)

Pop? . . . Pop? . . . I'm sorry, Pop. I didn't mean it like that. I'm sorry, okay?

POPS: Yeah, well, I'll tell you what: I'm fixin' to drop dead real soon—believe that—and when I go, you can throw yourself a fuckin' Shanghai Fiesta, and hire all the goddamn "1-800-BROTHER IN A SUIT" black attorneys that you want to—

JUNIOR: I said I was sorry—

POPS: Hurry up and become a fuckin' man already, Son—so I can break a hip and drop dead in peace.

JUNIOR: . . . I'll drop off the check. Don't mess with my box.

(Junior exits.)

POPS: . . . Oswaldo, gimme that damn butter knife from out the sink.

OSWALDO: For what? Not to open that box, right?

POPS: No. Not to open that box.

OSWALDO: So why you need the butter knife for?

POPS: Just go to the store, okay? Get that food for that always-hungry-heffer-church-lady before she get here and I got nothing to offer her, and then all she gonna do is talk the last good hearing out my ears with her boring heffer church lady talk . . . And bring me some Ritz crackers too—

OSWALDO: The low sodium kind, right?

POPS: Who say low sodium? Low sodium my ass! High sodium! The highest possible sodium. Get me the most extra-strength Ritz crackers the law allow, plus my Lotto tickets—and get the damn church lady's cookies and juice too—I don't wanna get caught empty-handed come Sunday.

OSWALDO: Okay, but I'm supposed to go to the Bronx now, could I bring it when I get back tonight?

POPS: What's in the Bronx?

OSWALDO: I visit people in the hospital, for like—amends and shit? Plus, I need to get my birth certificate for my job application, and it's up there at my father's place by Gun Hill Road.

POPS: Okay then.

OSWALDO: Plus, I mean the real reason is I need to go see my father. For like, to clear the air.

POPS: Just don't be late for supper. Invite your father if you want to.

OSWALDO: Nah, we don't got that type of relationship. He not like you. He old-school.

POPS: Who say I ain't old-school?

OSWALDO: You old-school yeah, but, you know, you different. He didn't never visit me when I was upstate, he didn't never even come to court. He, you know, he old-school. Like John Wayne—but Boriqua.

POPS: Well, when you go over there, bring him a little gift, like a coffee cake or something.

OSWALDO: I bought him a brand-new bad-ass Black Rhino twenty-eight-ounce framing hammer with the ergonomic grip from Home Depot. Also, I'm gonna give him my ninety-day NA chip. I told you I got my ninety-day NA chip?

POPS: You did. You making good progress, Oswaldo. I'm proud of you.

OSWALDO: Thanks, Dad.

POPS: And hey—what you was saying before about your case-worker saying that I get annoyed by you? He don't know shit.

OSWALDO: For real?

POPS: We breakfast buddies—ain't nothin' wrong with that.

(Pops stares at Junior's box.)

OSWALDO: Yes sir. Okay. Well, I'll see ya at dinner then. Love you, Dad.

POPS: Okay. Now, on your way out—hand me that damn butter knife.

SCENE 2

The Roof. The Same Day.

Lulu and Pops smoke pot.

POPS: Junior don't have to know nothing about this here chiba, right? I don't wanna set a bad example for his sobriety.

LULU: Junior's not sober. Oswaldo's sober. And I'm sober.

POPS: You smoking weed, Lulu—by definition, that means you ain't sober.

LULU: No but, me and my higher power, we have an under-standing. Besides I only smoke with you—and with Junior every once in awhile.

POPS: Junior don't smoke no weed. And I only smoke for that glaucoma.

LULU: Okay . . . .

POPS: . . . . . . Say, I was just wondering: you ever think about getting a trade, Lulu?

LULU: You mean like a job? But I'm a student, Dad.

POPS: . . . A student, yes. When you graduating?

LULU: Not for like, not for, but, like soon, or soon-ish . . . .
It's so pretty out this time of the day, isn't it?

POPS: . . . It is.

LULU: It reminds me of, like, a foreign land . . .

POPS: . . . What kinda foreign land?

LULU: I don't know . . . Like, *Game of Thrones* or something?? . . .
I really appreciate you taking me in, Dad.

POPS: You family, Lulu. Ain't a thing.

LULU: I'm pregnant. Junior says I can do what I want and he'll
support the decision, but I can really tell he doesn't want
me to have it.

POPS: . . . What?

LULU: What do you think? Do you think I should have it?

POPS: I'm a take you to the doctor, okay? Make sure you're okay.

LULU: Oh I'm fine.

POPS: Nah. I mean an obstetrician. A baby doctor. We got one
in the building—Doctor Shaw. He's a good man. We'll go
see him later today.

LULU: But I don't think Junior wants the baby.

POPS: Oh he wants the baby! And if he don't want it—I'll take
it. Raise it I mean. Whatever you need. I mean, the baby—
it's Junior's, right?

LULU: . . . . Dad?!

POPS: . . . Hey hey, no no, don't be upset, I apologize—that
was a real insensitive remark—of course the baby's Junior's.
Right?

LULU: I may look how I look—but that don't mean I *am* how
I look!

POPS: I know.

LULU: I'm gonna be a accountant some day!

POPS: And a mother. And I'm tickled pink, Lulu.

LULU: . . . So you'll talk to Junior for me when the time comes?

POPS: Oh hell yes, I'll talk to Junior tonight.

LULU: Not tonight though, okay? He'll be mad if he knows
I told you before, like, well, we just found out, ya know?

POPS: You just tell me when you need me to step in. But really? Once the idea settles inside of Junior, he'll come around. He loves kids—and kids—they gravitate to him naturally. Kids and pets. You should see him at a barbecue . . .

LULU: Also, I'll go to the doctor when you start taking your glaucoma and diabetes medicines. And your heart and blood pressure pills too . . . . . . And I watch you take them.

POPS: A grandchild . . . I hope it's a baby girl, but I bet it's gonna be a boy. Us Washingtons, we don't fire to the left, we straight-shooting men—we make sons.

LULU: Um so—we got a deal then, Dad?

POPS: Let's shake on it. We got a deal.

LULU: I love you, Dad!

POPS: Dass cuz I'm lovable.

LULU: I'll walk the dog before dinner.

POPS: Okay then.

LULU: Oh—you want the rest of this?

POPS: Hell no. And neither do you—we having a baby!

SCENE 3

Living Room. That Evening.

A dead Christmas tree is fully lit. Pops, Lulu, Junior, Detective O'Connor and her fiancé, Lieutenant Caro, drink beverages in the living room after dinner. Midstream:

LIEUTENANT CARO: . . . Okay, so, gorilla walks into a bar, orders a banana daiquiri—

LULU: That's funny!!!

LIEUTENANT CARO: Hold on, there's more. So: gorilla walks into a bar, orders a banana daiquiri, bartender gives him the banana daiquiri, says: "That'll be twenty-five dollars." Gorilla pays him, takes a sip of his drink. Bartender says:

"Hey, not for nothing, but we don't get a lot of gorillas in here." Gorilla says: "At these prices I'm not surprised!!"

DETECTIVE O'CONNOR: "At these prices!!"

LIEUTENANT CARO: And Mr. Washington—the perp who told me that one? My hand to God—he was completely naked and cuffed at the time—we had just nabbed him for public indecency!

POPS: Oh I believe it. Shoot, we had one guy—musta popped him a dozen times for whacking off in public—what'd we use to call him, Audrey?

DETECTIVE O'CONNOR: "Whacky-Whacky."

POPS: "Whacky-Whacky," thass right! Oriental fellow, very polite—just couldn't keep his pants on—

DETECTIVE O'CONNOR: Multiple trips to the psych ward, Dave—the guy just keeps repeat offending. Till one day, Walter here takes the guy aside, has a few words with him, then takes out his business card, writes a little note on it, sticks it in Whacky-Whacky's pocket—and after that—no more whacky-whacky.

LIEUTENANT CARO: What'd the note say, Mr. Washington?

POPS: Aw, you wouldn't believe me if I told you.

LULU: Tell us, Dad!

POPS: Well. Note said: "Home? Whacky-whacky. Not home? No whacky-whacky." I told him keep that note in his pocket 24/7 and refer to it at all times. And I guess it worked. He even got the shit laminated, remember Audrey?

LIEUTENANT CARO: You hear that Audrey—he got the note laminated! Laminated! Did you hear that, honey?

DETECTIVE O'CONNOR: I heard it, Dave—I was there, remember?

LIEUTENANT CARO: That's true—that's very true—

DETECTIVE O'CONNOR: How much wine did you have with dinner, sweetie?

POPS: Aw leave the man alone, Audrey!

LIEUTENANT CARO: Thank you, Mr. Washington! And speaking of thank-yous—that meal you cooked this evening, Mr. Washington—I mean, you really are one helluva incredible gourmet chef!

POPS: Well, 'bout a week after marrying my late wife, it became clear either I was gonna cook, or we was gonna starve— ain't that right, Audrey?

JUNIOR: Oh c'mon—Moms could cook a little!

POPS: Your mother was my superior in every area, Son, with the notable exception of the kitchen—

JUNIOR: C'mon, Pops, what about those things she made?! Whaddya call them tasty things—croquettes, bouquets— like fried fish all delicious with that sauce?

POPS: You mean fish sticks?

JUNIOR: They wasn't no fish sticks, these was handmade!

POPS: They was fish sticks with the fisherman right on the box!

JUNIOR: My moms could cook, Lulu.

LULU: I believe you.

JUNIOR: And that's on top of keeping house, and doing the parenting—and everything else she did with the church and the kids—

DETECTIVE O'CONNOR: Your father's just having fun, Junior—

JUNIOR: And she worked full-time just like you—and at a higher salary too.

DETECTIVE O'CONNOR: Well, all I know, Junior, is that your mother is looking down on you right now so proud for moving back in here and taking care of your father.

POPS: Taking care of me? He get free rent, all he can eat, cable-TV, internet computer, 'round-the-clock electricity, got all his friends flopping here like it's Section-8 housing, this ain't no kind of burden on him, this here is damn Shangri-la!

JUNIOR: Shangri-what?

DETECTIVE O'CONNOR: It's okay Junior, I get it.

LIEUTENANT CARO: Mr. Washington. Tell us that story Audrey always tells me 'bout when you were first partners—

DETECTIVE O'CONNOR: Oh God! Not Lawrence Taylor at the China Club!

LIEUTENANT CARO: No No! Mr. Washington—the knife guy— you know—Hell's Kitchen, the knife?!

POPS: Oh that ain't a nice story.

LULU: Tell it, Dad—please! Here, I'll pour you another drink.

LIEUTENANT CARO: Give the man a drink—yes! In fact, let me do the honors, I'll join you.

DETECTIVE O'CONNOR: Dave—

LIEUTENANT CARO: What—I'm gonna let him drink alone? Salud, Mr. Washington! Now, the story, please.

POPS: Aw I don't hardly even remember. Audrey was a rookie—

DETECTIVE O'CONNOR: My first week—

POPS: In other words, a danger to herself and others.

DETECTIVE O'CONNOR: It's true.

POPS: So, yeah—we rolled up, 45th and 10th, there's a damn brawl in the street—so I called in for backup—but Rocky Balboa here had other ideas—

DETECTIVE O'CONNOR: My blood was flowing, the adrenaline, some guy brushed me—

LIEUTENANT CARO: Oh she's the same today—you should see her at the checkout line at Trader Joe's—

DETECTIVE O'CONNOR: So I grabbed the guy good, but then he gets leverage, and starts swinging on me. So Walter came over beat the guy down.

POPS: I subdued him.

LIEUTENANT CARO: "Subdued"—absolutely!

DETECTIVE O'CONNOR: So Walter's subduing him, but then all of the sudden, I scream!—

LULU: Cuz why?

DETECTIVE O'CONNOR: Cuz the guy Walter's subduing—has got a knife in his head!

LIEUTENANT CARO: "Knife in his head!" —I fuckin' love this story!!

LULU: Like in his actual head?

DETECTIVE O'CONNOR: Yes. So I'm like: "Walter, knife in head. Knife in head!" Walter sees the knife in this guy's head, puts him in the squad car, tells him we're taking him to the ER—of course the guy's drunk out of his mind, and has no idea he's got a knife in his head.

LULU: Like, a real knife?

DETECTIVE O'CONNOR: Yes.

LULU: You heard that, baby? A knife.

JUNIOR: Uh-huh.

DETECTIVE O'CONNOR: So we get him in the car, Walter's driving, the siren—

POPS: Guy asks me for a cigarette. So I tell Audrey, reach into my pocket, give him one of my Kools.

LULU: With a knife in his head?!

DETECTIVE O'CONNOR: And I'm freaking out—because Walter, he actually slows the car down so I could light the guy's cigarette.

POPS: Then the motherfucker asks can we stop and grab him a Pepsi.

DETECTIVE O'CONNOR: Not Pepsi, beer! Drunk, bleeding out, blood everywhere, knife in his head, he wants a beer—

LIEUTENANT CARO: "Irish First Aid"—why not?!

POPS: You know it! So I pull over at the bodega, I say: "Audrey, go get this man a beer—in fact, get me one too."

DETECTIVE O'CONNOR: So what could I do—I got the beers.

POPS: Löwenbräu! They was nice and cold too.

DETECTIVE O'CONNOR: Anyway, finally—precious minutes lost—we pull up to the ER, tires squealing—but now the guy doesn't wanna leave his new best friend Walter! He's talking to Walter about horse racing, current events. And I'm, like: "Hey, come on, let's go!"

POPS: I told Audrey, let the man finish his beer.

DETECTIVE O'CONNOR: Again—what could I do? So he finishes the beer, we carry him in, hand him off to triage, but now I'm ready to go back to the precinct and report Walter to my captain—seconds were precious and he was wasting time giving the guy cigarettes and beer.

POPS: "One for the road"—know what I'm sayin', Dave?

LULU: Wait, I don't get it.

POPS: See, the man, Lulu, he was in shock from his injury—and the second they pulled that knife out from his head, he was only gonna just hemorrhage and be immediately dead.

Couldn't happen any other way. That's just the luck of the draw when you got a big knife in your head—or any foreign object embedded that deep for that matter. So I had a beer with him. The man was gonna die alone—I figured he didn't have to drink alone too. Ya know?

LIEUTENANT CARO: See, that's what we used to call: "Doing the wrong thing to do the right thing"—not like that no more, Mr. Washington, and it's a goddamn shame. Salud!

POPS: Salud.

LULU: But, wait—couldn't they just leave the knife in his head?

POPS: Um, no Lulu. I'm afraid they couldn't.

LIEUTENANT CARO: Your father, Junior, I never did have the pleasure to work with him, but everything Audrey tells me is nothing but he was one of the great ones—and I don't just hear that from Audrey. And by the way—your comment before about your father's take-home pay? You oughta keep in mind that when your father came up in the force in the late '70s—being a black guy didn't exactly put him on the fast track for career advancement, yet he served with distinction and valor. And to that I say once more: "Salud, Mr. Washington!"

POPS: Call me Walter.

LIEUTENANT CARO: I'd be honored to.

DETECTIVE O'CONNOR: You know I'm behind a desk now, Walter—Detective Specialist? And Dave here is a lieutenant, so—

POPS: Yep—I can see the brass.

LIEUTENANT CARO: I miss the action though, Walter. I'm a glorified paper shuffler now. Audrey had to put me on that Paleo Diet—all this inactivity, I mean I'm a guy who likes taking his shirt off when I wash the car or mow the lawn—you know what I mean?

POPS: Feel the sun on you.

LIEUTENANT CARO: Exactly. See honey, he knows.

DETECTIVE O'CONNOR: I miss you Walter. I miss those days coming up with you in the '90s. Granted it wasn't much fun to be a cop back then—

POPS: Fuckin' Giuliani—

LIEUTENANT CARO: Oh amen to that, Walter! You know, we had dinner with that miserable Giuliani cocksucker last week me and Audrey—a departmental brass thing—some crappy French place costs ten dollars for a Diet Coke. And do you know what that pretentious guinea windbag ordered? A fuckin' pigeon! A pigeon, Walter—like his shit don't stink! Like: "Ooo la la, bring me zee pigeon"—like he ain't the son of a two-bit Sing Sing ex-con from East Flatbush. I wanted to spit in his "foie gras" or whatever the fuck they call that overpriced duck grease they're slinging over there.

DETECTIVE O'CONNOR: Okay, Dave—

LIEUTENANT CARO: I mean we got a photo with him—but strictly for appearances, believe me.

DETECTIVE O'CONNOR: Anyway, what I was trying to say— Giuliani aside—

LIEUTENANT CARO: I'm sorry. Just hearing his name—it causes my rear end to do that sudden jabbing-startling what-the-fuck-just-happened-maybe-I-got-cancer sneak-attack ass-flinch thing. You know the one?

DETECTIVE O'CONNOR: Are you done? . . .

LIEUTENANT CARO: I'm done. And please forgive my profanity. And I won't even get into him sitting in the Yankee dug-out. The audacity, wearing the friggin' uniform like he's Joe Pepitone with a toupee—the jerk. Okay. I'm done now. God Bless Al Sharpton and Let's Go Mets.

DETECTIVE O'CONNOR: Anyway, my point, Walter, all kidding aside, I miss working with you, ya know? Those were good days.

POPS: Didn't turn out so good for me in the end though, now did it?

LIEUTENANT CARO: You caught a terrible break, Walter.

POPS: Shit. Fuck the NYPD—present company excluded.

JUNIOR: Okay then. Audrey, it was real nice seeing you again. I gotta catch a bus.

LIEUTENANT CARO: Very nice meeting you, Junior. Here, take my card, you know, like if you get stopped for a red light.

JUNIOR: I don't drive . . . Lulu, wanna walk me to the train?

LULU: Sure, baby.

JUNIOR: You gonna be alright, Pop, with Oswaldo and Lulu looking over things for a few days? Cuz I don't have to go—not at all.

POPS: Get your ass on that bus, Junior—hold up. Here.

JUNIOR: I got money.

POPS: Well now you got some more.

JUNIOR: I love you, Pop.

POPS: Don't get locked up.

LULU: Bye, Dad.

(*Junior and Lulu exit.*)

DETECTIVE O'CONNOR: She calls you "Dad," Walter?

POPS: They all call me that and I've given up objecting . . . So now, Audrey, Dave: what's this about you two getting married?

DETECTIVE O'CONNOR: You like the ring?

POPS: Yowza! Helluva rock—that musta set you back plenty, Dave.

LIEUTENANT CARO: Can't put a price tag on happiness, Walter.

POPS: That's what I like to hear. Still, I'm no jeweler, but this looks like some serious Audrey Hepburn–Cartier– Kim Kardashian–shit right here. You didn't rob a bank to make the down payment, did you?

LIEUTENANT CARO: Actually, I paid cash.

DETECTIVE O'CONNOR: Tell him, Dave.

LIEUTENANT CARO: I play a little poker, Walter.

DETECTIVE O'CONNOR: Don't be modest.

LIEUTENANT CARO: Okay, I play a lot of poker. Well, I used to. Audrey and I attended a charity tournament—one of those things you can't get out of?

DETECTIVE O'CONNOR: Well Dave got out of there—with over thirty thousand dollars.

LIEUTENANT CARO: There was a game after the game, I beat a major "A-list" Hollywood celebrity for thirty large.

POPS: Who was it?

LIEUTENANT CARO: His only stipulation was that I could never tell.

DETECTIVE O'CONNOR: It was Ben Affleck!

POPS: Who's that?

LIEUTENANT CARO: He's a guy, Walter. That's the thing, they're all just guys. Anyway, the next morning, I took Audrey directly to Tiffany's, told the gal behind the counter; "I got thirty grand to spend and I don't want a penny change."

DETECTIVE O'CONNOR: And he hasn't played poker since.

LIEUTENANT CARO: That she knows of. Just kidding. No really, I'm kidding.

DETECTIVE O'CONNOR: I mean it's just a ring, but, I adore it—and it will be a good story some day for the grandkids.

POPS: Funny you should mention that. I got some news too. Seems I'm gonna be a grandfather.

LIEUTENANT CARO: Hey, congratulations!

DETECTIVE O'CONNOR: Oh Walter! Walter, Oh my God! A grandfather! Finally! And Junior, he didn't even say a word!

POPS: We just found out today actually, so, you know—

DETECTIVE O'CONNOR: Of course! Oh Walter! Walter!

POPS: Not bad, huh?

DETECTIVE O'CONNOR: Delores would have already built the crib by hand and wallpapered the baby's room.

POPS: Yeah, she woulda. She up there smiling though.

DETECTIVE O'CONNOR: Yes she is. Wow. Oh my God. That is the best news I've heard in—wow . . . And hey, you know what? I think on that joyous note—

LIEUTENANT CARO: Say, I could use a bit more coffee, Walter, if you can spare it.

DETECTIVE O'CONNOR: Um, I think we really should let Walter get some rest, Dave.

LIEUTENANT CARO: Long drive back to the Island, honey. Walter, you mind if Audrey here gets me a refill on the coffee before we take off?

DETECTIVE O'CONNOR: It's late, Dave, I really think—

POPS: Audrey. It's okay. I'd like a coffee too if you don't mind. With a shot of cognac. You want a shot of cognac, Dave?

LIEUTENANT CARO: Just the coffee. And, um—maybe just one more of those apple fritters? It's okay I eat another fritter?

DETECTIVE O'CONNOR: It's time to go, honey.

LIEUTENANT CARO: Audrey—

DETECTIVE O'CONNOR: I said it's time to go.

POPS: Hey hey, no bickering on my account. Dave: why don't you just say whatever it is you've obviously come here to say, and then, you can take all the coffee and fritters you want to go on your way back to Long Island—how's that sound?

DETECTIVE O'CONNOR: Oh God—we came here to help you, I came here to help you, I would never—

POPS: It's all good, Audrey. Let your man say what he need to say.

LIEUTENANT CARO: Do I really need to say it? . . . . . . Okay. You gotta drop this civil suit and settle, Walter. It's an election year. And the mayor's office is already catching enough flack off of this bogus Williams shooting.

POPS: Yeah, I read about that one. Seems the department hasn't gotten any better at not shooting at innocent black men.

LIEUTENANT CARO: Hey, I hear you, Walter, don't think I don't, but I mean, if I may, what are you holding out for after how many—eight—years already? Eight years, Walter— I mean, your lawyers, what? The phrase "strike while the iron's hot," that's like—an old wives' tale to them?

POPS: My lawyers act on my instructions.

LIEUTENANT CARO: You're a proud man, I get it. And eight years ago, when you were in the newspapers every day, public opinion running high, the outrage, the call for justice—then absolutely, hold out for all you can get off those bastards—but now? The truth is nobody cares about your case anymore except you—and maybe the *Village Voice*. And Walter, who the fuck reads the *Village Voice* these days?! Look, do yourself a favor. Sign the nondisclosure. Cash a check with a little weight to it. Live your life a happy man instead of—

POPS: Instead of what?

LIEUTENANT CARO: C'mon. You're gonna lose this apartment first off, that's number one.

DETECTIVE O'CONNOR: Walter, you've been served with multiple subpoenas already, from your landlord, no?

POPS: How you know about that?

DETECTIVE O'CONNOR: They'll toss you out of here, Walter. You're paying fifteen hundred a month for a palatial mansion on Riverside Drive worth ten times that—you don't think they want you out of here?

POPS: I got a lease and it's legal—

DETECTIVE O'CONNOR: Walter, I read the affidavits. When Delores was alive, you had a clean and upstanding home and you had leverage with the city because they had nothing on you. But since she's passed, Walter, you've brought undo attention to yourself with unsavory characters, pot-smoking complaints, bottles thrown out windows, vandalism, weird strangeness, criminal allegations—all violations to the terms of your lease. The city takes notice of these things, Walter, and now they're the ones with the leverage, they need your case to go away, and unfortunately, you gave them their opening.

LIEUTENANT CARO: But they can't do shit and won't do shit if they receive the right call from downtown. Come on, Walter—you think we like landlords?! Who likes landlords?! Fuck landlords!! We're on your side!

DETECTIVE O'CONNOR: You need to settle. Trust me. And trust Dave: he's only here trying to help me look out for you.

POPS: "Trust Dave," huh?

DETECTIVE O'CONNOR: Walter, please, we're here to help—

LIEUTENANT CARO: No, Audrey, Walter's absolutely right. But the thing is, Walter—the city means business here—and we both know that no one beats City Hall, however, there's a way to handle this where everybody wins and it doesn't have to get ugly—

POPS: How's it gonna get ugly?

LIEUTENANT CARO: C'mon, Walter—I think you know the answer to that question.

POPS: Get the fuck out my house, motherfucker—how's that for an answer?!

LIEUTENANT CARO: Okay. First of all—and believe me I would never do this—but we both know I could lock you up right now as an accessory to grand larceny for the little "discount store" your son is running out of his bedroom—second room on the left, right? No disrespect, Walter—but what's the chances I go into that room right now and don't find a bunch of electronical items without the proper receipts?

DETECTIVE O'CONNOR: He gets the point, Dave—

LIEUTENANT CARO: Or how about I go into the next room by the bathroom—where the other convicted felon lives? Or how about I make an inquiry into your son's girlfriend, Walter—because I'll eat my hat if she ain't a pro and for all we know Junior is her pimp—

POPS: I was a highly decorated cop—

LIEUTENANT CARO: You weren't. I'm sorry. You weren't a highly decorated cop. You were an okay cop. Better than some, no worse than some others. No shame in that. Be smart. Take the money. Eight years ago, you caught a bad break—

POPS: "Bad break"?! When's the last time a black cop shot a fuckin' white cop six times "accidentally"—and they chalked it up as a "bad break"?!

LIEUTENANT CARO: There was a hearing, Walter, you were present, the officer was disciplined to the severest degree short of termination—

POPS: Yeah, and my black ass is still chock-full of the bullet holes his white rookie–ass plugged up in me, now isn't it?!

LIEUTENANT CARO: Yes, Walter. He's white. You're black.

POPS: Goddamn right I'm black!

LIEUTENANT CARO: No one's saying you aren't black. Who's saying you're not black? No one's saying anything about anything—except to offer you a settlement you should've taken eight years ago. We're all cops here, Walter, right? No black, no white—just blue.

POPS: This ain't about no black, white or blue—this is about the green, Jack—and if I was white, they woulda given me my five million years ago!

LIEUTENANT CARO: Forgive me, Walter, but you're dreaming.

POPS: Was I dreaming when that boy called me "nigger" before he shot me full of holes?

DETECTIVE O'CONNOR: That's an unsubstantiated allegation, Walter.

POPS: Oh so now I'm some liar crying "nigger" for a payday?!

LIEUTENANT CARO: Hey, man, calm down. Believe me, we came here as a courtesy.

POPS: I know full well why you came here—any opportunity to curry favor with the bosses! Bet it went something like this: "Yes, sir, Boss: my fiancée was his partner. So I can get that Old Bitter Monkey-Ass Nigger to sign that nondisclosure, cuz I'm like the Horse Whisperer of Getting Niggers to Sign Shit!

DETECTIVE O'CONNOR: Wow.

LIEUTENANT CARO: Nah, hey, I get it, and I get you, Walter— more than you think. And I take no offense. And personally, I would love to be able to agree with you completely. Because if not for the fact that you happen to be totally wrong, you'd probably be right. And I mean that. And that being said, I'm certain that you'll also have to agree with me that— whether we like it or not—the simple fact is that not every- thing in this world, Walter, is about being fuckin' black!

DETECTIVE O'CONNOR: David!

POPS: It's okay, Audrey, I been dealing with these folks all my life.

LIEUTENANT CARO: "These folks," right, of course, exactly—

DETECTIVE O'CONNOR: Walter, do you honestly believe I could ever be engaged to a man who would ever think like you described—much less speak like that?

POPS: I don't know, Audrey, it's been awhile . . . And you wrong, Dave: it is about being black. Always has been, always will be—and who the fuck are you to try and tell a black man otherwise?

LIEUTENANT CARO: I apologize. But Walter, I'm telling you: don't be the Old Black Man in the New White World. It's a decent settlement. Cut your losses and take it. Let's go, Audrey.

POPS: Hey, Caro: you're gonna go home and jump into bed with my old partner here tonight, right?

LIEUTENANT CARO: I don't see what that's got to do with anything—

POPS: And if you got any pep left in your step, you gonna make love before you roll over and go to sleep and dream about being promoted up the damn "Alpo dog food" police chain, now aren't you?

DETECTIVE O'CONNOR: Walter—

POPS: You still get it up, don't ya, Lieutenant?

LIEUTENANT CARO: I'm a man, Walter—of course I get it up.

POPS: Well I don't! The last eight years of my wife's life—after the shooting—I couldn't do nothing with her 'cept drink tea and play Scrabble if you get my meaning—and that ain't the half of it.

LIEUTENANT CARO: I'm very sorry for that Walter.

POPS: Not as sorry as me and my wife, motherfucker—believe that!!!

DETECTIVE O'CONNOR: And whose fault is that really, Walter?

POPS: . . . Excuse me, Audrey?

LIEUTENANT CARO: You're about to lose your apartment and believe me, a whole lot more if they decide to unleash forensic accountants on every financial transaction you've ever made—not to mention what they could do to your three-quarter pension if they put every arrest you ever filed in thirty years under a microscope.

POPS: I wanna know what you meant before, Audrey, when you said: "Whose fault is that really, Walter?"

LIEUTENANT CARO: Hey—they will arrest your son, that's definite—they might even try to arrest you. Why let them do that? For what? Because you're "right"? Sign the nondisclosure. Cash a check. Take a trip to Acapulco, the Poconos—your veal it was impeccable, maybe open up a little place, or not—

POPS: Audrey! What did you mean by: "Whose fault is that really?"!

DETECTIVE O'CONNOR: I'm on your side, Walter. But there are many people—black *and* white—who don't see this case the way that you do.

POPS: And are you one of those people?

DETECTIVE O'CONNOR: I wasn't there.

POPS: So some incompetent white-rookie–Justin Bieber motherfucker shoots me six times—empties his gun inside of me—and him doing that is my fault?!

DETECTIVE O'CONNOR: I misspoke, Walter, I'm sorry—

LIEUTENANT CARO: She misspoke, man—

POPS: You need to back up what you said, Audrey.

DETECTIVE O'CONNOR: . . . Or what?

POPS: Oh—so it's like that now?

(Lieutenant Caro advances toward Pops.)

LIEUTENANT CARO: Walter, c'mon—

POPS: Hey! Don't you come up on me!

DETECTIVE O'CONNOR: The night you got shot, Walter—you were off duty, you never ID'd yourself as a police officer, and your blood alcohol level was one for the record books!

POPS: So I got good and stinkin' drunk on my own dime, on my own time, and then the white rookie comes, opens fire on me—and that's my fault?!

DETECTIVE O'CONNOR: In an after-hours bar at six in the morning, populated with hookers, pimps and violent felons—a bar that was flagged by our precinct as a no-fly zone for cops—

POPS: You think I was associating? You think those criminals were my friends?

DETECTIVE O'CONNOR: I have no doubt whatsoever that there wasn't a person in that club that you didn't hold in complete contempt—including yourself, Walter.

POPS: The person I hold in contempt is you, Audrey—you and Lieutenant Ass Lick over there—so save the Dr. Phil "I don't like myself" bullshit for somebody else. "I don't like myself"?! Show me one cop who actually does his job, sees what we see, becomes what the streets make us become—show me one cop who did what I did for thirty years who "likes" himself!

LIEUTENANT CARO: Okay now, emotions are running high—

POPS: Everybody hates fuckin' cops—even cops hate cops. And everybody especially don't like black cops! White cops were never comfortable with us, black civilians think we Uncle Tom, white civilians think we uppity, and everybody damn else sees we're black and thinks we're somehow not entirely qualified to carry a badge and a gun—

DETECTIVE O'CONNOR: Walter—

POPS: "Do I like myself"? Hell no! Do I drink? Hell yes! Thirty years, I gave everything to the job, and you got the nerve to come at me with: "Whose fault is that really, Walter?" That white rookie opened fire on me, Audrey! And he called me "nigger" while he did it. Six shots—N.I.G.G.E.R.—that's what that was! He shot everything black in the whole joint and somehow didn't hit anything white. Now how the fuck is that possible—and don't I have the same right as anybody else to sip on a damn margarita and not get shot the fuck up in the process?

DETECTIVE O'CONNOR: It's not your fault that he shot you, Walter. It's your fault that you were there. You clocked out at

STEPHEN ADLY GUIRGIS

nine P.M. that night. Bars close at four. Seven hours wasn't enough for you?

POPS: I drink sometimes. And I pay my own way when I do.

DETECTIVE O'CONNOR: And you paid an awful lot for those last few drinks that night, didn't you? "Whose fault was it?" It was the rookie's. "Whose fault was it really?" I can't answer that. But I know Delores, your wife, had an opinion on that subject. Because if you didn't have to be at an after-hours bar at six A.M., this never would've happened. But you did have to be there, didn't you? And, Walter, if I walk outta here right now and a safe falls on my head, it's not my fault. But if a safe falls on my head when I'm dead drunk at six in the morning, hanging out in a location where safes are known to sometimes drop on heads—

LIEUTENANT CARO: Walter, just, if I may: about the settlement—

POPS: Fuck your settlement, Caro!

LIEUTENANT CARO: Walter, please: this is all my fault and this is not how this evening was supposed to go. And you're right, I am a department suck-up—I got my eye on a much higher pay-grade and I'll choke on brass cock to get there. Whatever it takes. But the thing is, I'm in love with this woman here. I love her Walter—and all I know is she wants you to walk her down that aisle on our wedding day, which means I want that too. Think this through. Please . . . Look, my father was a patrolman just like you. He wasn't black, obviously, but he was like you. He was a lot like you. Not the best, not the worst. Just the salt of the earth, ya know? And the job ends up killing us one way or the other. Often literally. My dad—he ate his gun, okay? You woulda liked him. And him you. So even though I don't know, I know a little. Sign the nondisclosure. Don't be a martyr. Be a grandfather. They'll need your answer by five P.M. Monday, Walter.

DETECTIVE O'CONNOR: Please, Walter.

POPS: I got an answer right now: Fuck all a y'all. They wanna hang me from a cross—hang me. Ten dollars, ten million

dollars—I don't give a fuck. Just make sure you tell who-
ever sent you that Walter Washington is a man. They ain't
crucifying some supernatural Jesus!

(They exit.)

Walter Washington's a flesh-and-blood, pee-standing-up,
registered Republican—

*(Pops coughs, then staggers, steadies himself, then collapses—and
drinks. Pops is dimly lit throughout the following:)*

SCENE 4

The Roof. Immediately After Dinner.

Lulu and Junior smoke a joint. Junior has a suitcase by his side.

LULU: . . . It really is so pretty up here this time of night.
JUNIOR: I gotta go, Lulu.
LULU: . . . Hey, remember when we fucked on that water tower
    and I almost fell off?
JUNIOR: Yeah.
LULU: Let's do it again.
JUNIOR: I gotta catch my bus now.
LULU: I don't know why I can't go to Baltimore with you, Junior.
JUNIOR: I just need a coupla days alone.
LULU: Yeah, but I could go with you and you could still be alone.
JUNIOR: Yeah but I'll be more alone if I'm actually alone.
LULU: But why you have to be alone?
JUNIOR: Don't you ever like to be alone?
LULU: No.
JUNIOR: When I met you, you were alone.
LULU: I wasn't alone then. You thought I was alone, but I wasn't.

JUNIOR: Okay, but I like to be alone sometimes. Especially now with my Pops and all. Lulu, I gotta go, baby. I'm gonna miss the bus. I'll miss you. Believe me. I'll miss you a lot.

LULU: No you won't.

JUNIOR: I will too . . . Lulu? . . . Oh okay, c'mon—let's make love before we go to Broadway, okay?

LULU: You don't really wanna.

JUNIOR: Of course I wanna.

LULU: Well, I don't wanna.

JUNIOR: Why not?

LULU: Cuz before.

JUNIOR: Cuz before what?

LULU: Cuz before, I said to you that: "You thought I was alone, but I wasn't really alone," and you didn't react or nothing, you just said you wanted to be alone, like you weren't jealous or nothing!

JUNIOR: That's not true. I heard what you said, and I made a mental note to fuck with you about it later, but for right now I just want us to be cool before I get on the bus.

LULU: Six months ago, you woulda been mad jealous. Six months ago you woulda never got on that bus. But now I'm pregnant and all you want is that I should get an abortion and kill our baby.

JUNIOR: I never said that. What I said was the decision was yours.

LULU: But your meaning was very clear! I bet you got some bitch in Baltimore anyway, don't you? I wish you did have a bitch over there, because I would cut a bitch and not even blink—even in my pregnant condition, which, you don't even care about that anyway.

JUNIOR: Lulu.

LULU: You said you was different, Junior! And I believed you! But thass okay, I know that's just what old men say to get young-girl pussy.

JUNIOR: Look, just be sure to walk the dog while I'm away, okay?

LULU: "Walk the dog"?! Are you fuckin' serious?

JUNIOR: Lulu—

LULU: "Lulu walk the dog," "Lulu fix me eggs," "Lulu get me weed," "Lulu suck on my dick"—

JUNIOR: Okay, calm yourself—

LULU: I been with drug dealers and murderers treated me better than you! I been with crackhead-homeless in Van Cortlandt Park half naked in a blizzard who showed me more love!

JUNIOR: Well go be with them then! I'm already taking care of one impossible goddamn child, Lulu—my father—and I ain't leaving him all alone even if it fuckin' kills me, but I got no space to take care of two!

LULU: I'm not killing our baby!

JUNIOR: I'm not talking about the baby, I'm talking about you!

LULU: . . . Do you love me—yes or no?!

JUNIOR: See this is exactly what I'm talking about—

LULU: Yes or no?!

JUNIOR: Yes!

LULU: "In love"—or just "love"?

JUNIOR: Both!

LULU: No you don't. This is over. We're through!

JUNIOR: . . . Hey, hey. C'mon. C'mon, Lulu. You know what? I'm fuckin' retarded.

LULU: Clearly.

JUNIOR: No, I mean—you wanna go to Baltimore, let's just go to Baltimore, okay? . . . Let's just go to Baltimore—c'mon, I'm serious. Let's go. But we gotta leave right now.

LULU: I don't wanna anymore.

JUNIOR: Okay, please? . . . Will you please go to Baltimore with me, baby? . . . Please? . . . I'm begging you, baby, I'm so stupid, I'm high on reefer I wouldn't even be smoking if my Pops wasn't so damn difficult, and let's just—would you please go to Baltimore with me—please? It won't be the same without you . . . Okay? Please?

LULU: . . . No.

JUNIOR: Okay, don't go.

LULU: Oh, okay, I guess I'll go. Let me just go downstairs and get my bag.

JUNIOR: You don't have time to pack—

LULU: Oh, I'm packed.

JUNIOR: You're what?

LULU: I love you so much, Junior. I love you so much, it makes me break out like I don't know—like I got chlamydia or something!

JUNIOR: You're fuckin' crazy, you know that, right?

LULU: Uh-huh. Kiss me. Kiss me now.

(They kiss.)

SCENE 5

Pops Is in the Same Position as Before, Drinking Heavily.

A record like the Chi-Lites' "Have You Seen Her" plays on the old record player. Pops drunkenly attempts to sing along.
Oswaldo enters, he is drunk.

OSWALDO: Hey, Dad, I missed dinner—but I brought you, where is that shit, I brought you, you gonna like it a lot— oh, I think I left it on the bus—

POPS: Is that you, Oswaldo?

OSWALDO: Yeah, it's—uh-oh—

(Oswaldo throws up on the floor.)

Oh man. Sorry about that. Fuck. That's disgraceful. I'm sorry, Dad.

POPS: You eat something bad, Oswaldo? Some bad fish maybe?

OSWALDO: I seen my father tonight, my real father. In the Bronx. I told you that before, right? It didn't go well.

POPS: It didn't?

OSWALDO: He told me I was no good. He told me I was a arrogant, petty fuck. He told me I was a bad fuckin' person, a scumbag. He told me I was a weak addict just circling the drain, then he told me get the fuck out and don't ever come back—can you believe that, Dad? He hit me in my face—see? He told me I was a First-Class Piece of Shit of the Highest Order. I don't think that was right—do you, Dad?

POPS: Nah, Oswaldo—that ain't right at all.

OSWALDO: Then he took my Black Rhino claw hammer with the ergonomics an' shit that I gave him—and I mean, I don't even know—I just fuckin' ran—you know? Anyway. As a result of this, I'm thinking about calling an escort service now, Dad—whatchu think about that?

POPS: . . . Oswaldo? Oswaldo—are you drunk, Oswaldo?

OSWALDO: They got these services now, you can get cocaine *and* a woman, like both, you know? Like one-stop shopping? I just need a few hundred bucks—I could borrow that from you, right, Dad?

POPS: Oswaldo, what's got into you?!

OSWALDO: Lemme just hold your credit card for a minute.

POPS: Hey! Now you sit your ass down.

OSWALDO: Your credit card. Lemme get it.

POPS: Hey now! I ain't gonna tell you again—

OSWALDO: You hit me!

POPS: I'm just backing you off—

OSWALDO: But you hit me, Dad.

POPS: Oswaldo—

OSWALDO: Why you hit me for? Why you being like that?

POPS: I'm, I'm sorry—

OSWALDO: No you ain't!

POPS: Oswaldo—

OSWALDO: Nah, Dad—just gimme your fuckin' credit card!

POPS: Hey now calm down.

OSWALDO: Credit card!

POPS: But it's me, Oswaldo—

OSWALDO: Why you acting like this for?! Credit card, Dad!
Credit card! Credit card! Credit card! Credit—Or debit!

(Blackout.)

ACT TWO

SCENE 1

Sunday Evening. Two Weeks Later.

The living room is in ruins. But the Christmas tree is still up and lit. Moving boxes are strewn about. Stuff broken. Pops has a dirty bandage above his eye and is now holding a cane. He sits on the couch, drinking bourbon he pours from a half-gallon bottle as he watches Lulu serve juice and cookies to a beautiful woman dressed all in black, wearing both a large Catholic cross and a beaded Brazilian Condomblé necklace.

LULU: Now there's plenty more cookies and juice if you want more, miss.

CHURCH LADY: Obrigado! That's very kind.

LULU: Like, "mucho, mucho!"

CHURCH LADY: Yes.

LULU: And, Dad, Junior says he's gotta lay low at Little Dirty's in East Flatbush until things blow over here—

POPS: Junior?! Junior who?! Been gone thirteen days now, he can't even pick up a damn phone?!

LULU: Yeah, he's a little upset by, like, things—but anyway I was thinking, I'd go out there now to visit with him? But then be back home and watch *Jeopardy* on the DVR with you like at midnight?

POPS: Just leave your keys with the elevator man—I don't wanna have to be getting up and down every time them moving people be ringing the doorbell—

LULU: Oh, and Junior also said we don't have to be moving out right now, Dad—that it takes awhile to get evicted.

POPS: Well I ain't trying to jostle you around once you're nine months pregnant with my grandchild. We gonna be out sooner or later—might as well be now . . . She having a baby—you know—a "bambino"?

CHURCH LADY: Oh! Beautiful!

LULU: I know, right?! . . . Okay, so, Dad—would you like to give me money or something so I can give it to Junior?

POPS: Junior's a grown man, Lulu.

LULU: Okay . . .

POPS: And Lulu—take the damn dog with you, okay? In fact, leave his ass in Brooklyn if the little motherfucker gets distracted and you can give him the slip.

LULU: Okay. Love you.

(Lulu exits. Beat.)

CHURCH LADY: . . . This girl? Very nice.

POPS: Yeah—she okay.

CHURCH LADY: No pregnant though.

POPS: Nah see, she ain't showing cuz it's only been a matter of days.

CHURCH LADY: Pregnant some day? Maybe. Pregnant today? No.

POPS: You a midwife or something?

CHURCH LADY: Sometimes, yes. But I can be wrong. Forgive me.

POPS: Well I hope you are.

CHURCH LADY: Yes. Me too . . . So please: are you sure I cannot bring you a fresh—how you say—bandage—for your eye?

POPS: I'm fine. Like I said, we had a little burglary here the other week, no big deal.

CHURCH LADY: Yes. But please, what is "burglary"?

POPS: It's a robbery? Um: "banditos locos"?

CHURCH LADY: Ladrao?! Ay! And you were alone?

POPS: I was. But the elevator man, Mr. Chico—he a friend of mine, and he seen this bandito come in, so Mr. Chico came upstairs to check on me, and Mr. Chico—well, he don't play.

CHURCH LADY: He defeated "bandito"?

POPS: Bandito left here in handcuffs, with several of his front teeth scattered over there by that houseplant. Bandito was lucky the police came. He was, well, he was a drug addict— you know how that goes.

CHURCH LADY: You knew the bandito?

POPS: I thought I knew him. But who really knows anybody anyway, ya know?

CHURCH LADY: I see you like to drink.

POPS: On occasion—this being one. Can I pour you a glass?

CHURCH LADY: I drink only on holidays.

POPS: Do Sundays qualify?

CHURCH LADY: You tempt me—but no . . . So . . . Ay! I'm eating all your cookies!

POPS: That's what they there for. You should see when Glenda, the lady who usually comes from the church, when she arrive, she go through two rolls of Chip Ahoys and a half gallon of juice before she even sit down almost.

CHURCH LADY: It must be great shock to you about Glenda falling ill.

POPS: Terrible shock, yes. Is she expected to survive?

CHURCH LADY: Oh yes, but she need to rest.

POPS: Well you tell her for me: rest for a long time.

CHURCH LADY: You're very close to Glenda?

POPS: You know, she began visiting my late wife when she got infirm, that was last year, and after Delores passed before Christmas, well, Glenda—she just kept on coming.

CHURCH LADY: Well, I'm sorry for you to be stuck with me.

POPS: Hey, a pretty young lady eating cookies in my kitchen ain't never gonna be what I consider to be "stuck."

CHURCH LADY: You think I'm pretty?

POPS: Oh, I don't mean nothin' by it, just—

CHURCH LADY: I have good skin, but I'm not pretty—or young.

POPS: You sell yourself short. And I bet your man agrees.

CHURCH LADY: I don't have man.

POPS: Every woman needs a man. Even some men, they need a man too.

CHURCH LADY: I don't need no man. I had one husband. God took him.

POPS: I'm sorry.

CHURCH LADY: Believe me, I thank God every day.

POPS: I like you.

CHURCH LADY: I like you too. Now tell me why you refuse to take communion from Glenda every week? Is because you angry at God? Because the holy truth, the sacred truth, the truth of the earth—is God loves you very much. I meet you for only ten minutes, I already see you are much loved by God. I see it, I feel it.

POPS: What makes you feel it?

CHURCH LADY: Sometime, I feel things deeply. And I see things. Like with you. I see you have an old soul.

POPS: I got an old everything.

CHURCH LADY: Yes. You make joke—to push me back, no? Okay. We can talk about weather if you want to. Sunny today, cloudy tomorrow—but you do believe I feel things, don't you?

POPS: I'm just trying to pass the time, quite frankly.

CHURCH LADY: I've upset you, I'm sorry. I should go.

POPS: What was your husband's name?

CHURCH LADY: Bernardo.

POPS: What'd he do?

CHURCH LADY: In our country, he was champion boxer.

POPS: My father was a sparring partner for Sugar Ray Robinson.

CHURCH LADY: Oh—and he is still living, yes?

POPS: Don't think so, but I never met the man, so I wouldn't know.

CHURCH LADY: I have two childrens. One son, one daughter. She live in Jackson Heights. And he, he is a wanderer.

POPS: I shoulda been a wanderer . . . What, why you smiling for?

CHURCH LADY: Because, Mr. Washington—you are a wanderer.

POPS: Is that something you "feel"?

CHURCH LADY: I feel a lot of things.

POPS: On account of them beads around your neck, right? That's some Santeria witchcraft paraphernalia, ain't it?

CHURCH LADY: Candomblé. How did you know?

POPS: Oh, I know shit.

CHURCH LADY: Because you were a cop?

POPS: Glenda told you about that, huh?

CHURCH LADY: No. I know shit too. But I can't tell you what I know unless you want me to. Shall I continue?

POPS: . . . I mean, am I free to speak my mind here?

CHURCH LADY: "Always we are free," Mr. Washington. Devils chase us, but "always we are free."

POPS: Devils, yes. See, I want to be fair because I like you. Now, I don't know exactly what you're after here, and I don't mind that you're after it—but, to be fair—what you don't know—is that you're messin' with the exact wrong motherfucker when it comes to that hoo-doo, voo-doo, boo-boo and doo-doo bullshit you're trying to front on me now.

CHURCH LADY: So I shouldn't tell you what I know?

POPS: Hey, it's your dime, sister—you wanna do a little magic show, bring it on, tell me what you know.

CHURCH LADY: I know you was fond of the bandito who did the burglary to you. I know he caused the wound above your eye. I know you love your son but he causes you shame and it shames you three times because you feel your shame, and his, plus more shame for feeling shame, no? And I know you're angry—so angry—that your wife passed—

POPS: Of course I'm angry my wife passed—what kinda decent husband wouldn't be angry 'bout that?

CHURCH LADY: Because God made her sick?

POPS: God didn't cause her illness—and he couldn't cure it neither.

CHURCH LADY: And I know when your wife Delores died, it was, in part—because she needed to leave you—

POPS: Now hold up now—

CHURCH LADY: And you were relieved when Delores passed, weren't you? Because you still loved her in your way, and she in hers, but you was no longer in love with each other. And you blame yourself for that—and for the prostitutes—

POPS: Prostitutes?!

CHURCH LADY: Prostitutes, yes! Were you not with prostitutes? Many prostitutes? I don't judge. In a bad time, I was prostitute in my country. Okay? But God is big—and "always we are free."

POPS: Who the hell sent you here?

CHURCH LADY: Maybe I was called here. By who, I don't know. But I'm here now. And I know there are people out there who want to hurt you. And you need protection. And I know, Mr. Washington—that you want to take communion with me—and that it will restore you fully. "Always we are free"—Mr. Washington. Always. Take communion with me, Mr. Washington.

POPS: Look here: I ain't for no communion, I ain't for that old-slave religion—and I ain't for none of this "always we are free," and this "somehow you know every damn thing" business neither.

CHURCH LADY: I thought you were a serious man.

POPS: I am.

CHURCH LADY: And I am serious woman. These beads, this cross, they are serious. They mean something. The communion wafer, it means something too.

POPS: To you it does, and I respect that. You here to visit the elderly, right? Well, visit with me a minute—just knock off the jungle boogie. Now, where you live at?

CHURCH LADY: For to make "chitchat"? Okay. Two months in New York, I clean for the church. The other ten, in a favela in São Paolo. I volunteer at an orphanage there, it borders the leper colony.

POPS: Hold up—they got lepers over there? I thought they was extinct?

(She laughs.)

CHURCH LADY: That's funny.

POPS: I'm sorry—I didn't mean it to be.

CHURCH LADY: Funny man. Strong man.

POPS: So I been told.

CHURCH LADY: You won't take communion, Strong Man—even just for me?

POPS: We been through that already. Now say, where you from again?

CHURCH LADY: "Chitchat, chitchat," eh? Okay. Brazil. I come from there.

POPS: Okay. So now let me ask you, Miss Brazil: can't y'all appreciate even one tiny friendly evening drink over there in Brazil?

CHURCH LADY: God still loves you, Mr. Washington. Don't be too proud to be free. "Always we are free." God loves you. And your life can be, believe me, a beautiful life indeed if you can only learn to love God back.

POPS: Oh cut the shit, will ya! There is no God. And if somehow there is, well—

CHURCH LADY: Well what?

POPS: Well give me five minutes and a fair fight, and I'll show God exactly what I think of him.

CHURCH LADY: I can heal you.

POPS: I ain't sick.

CHURCH LADY: You don't have to believe me, you just have to let me.

POPS: You can't heal shit!

CHURCH LADY: I coming closer now. Look at me. Don't be scare. Walter. Look at me.

(He does. Beat. She stares at him intently, as if in a trance.)

I can heal you.

(Beat. Pops is in the grips of intense energy, almost frozen, but trying to resist.)

POPS: No one can heal me.

CHURCH LADY: I can. I'm here for dat. I'm here for God. I'm here for you.

(She removes her cross and beaded necklace and loosens her hair and her dress. Pops is transfixed.)

I can baptize you.

(Pops can't move. She takes the bourbon, pours it wildly on her face and down her throat. She pours it into Pops's mouth as well—a waterfall of bourbon.)

POPS: You can't heal me—I won't be healed.

CHURCH LADY: You are healing.

(They come together and grow intimate. It's ritualistic and sexual, but also it's not. It's intense and growing more so.
 Pops becomes aware that—inexplicably—he is aroused down below.)

POPS: This is impossible.

CHURCH LADY: "Always we are free"—you are free.

POPS: But this shit is impossible.

CHURCH LADY: You are free.

(The Church Lady puts a Eucharist wafer between her teeth, mounts Walter, and feeds it to him mouth to mouth.)

POPS: I'm having difficulty breathing.

CHURCH LADY: You took communion, Walter! So wonderful.

POPS: Oh. Oh my.

(The Church Lady remains on top of him and inserts him into her. They make love slowly, quietly, throughout.)

This is impossible.

CHURCH LADY: Why?

POPS: I mean medically—this is medically—I'm talking medically— Oh my Lord—

CHURCH LADY: Pai Nosso, que estás no céu, Santificado seja o Teu Nome— Be free, Walter.

POPS: Free, yes, I'm very free.

CHURCH LADY: Santa, Santa! Negrinho do Pastoreio! Bumba-meu-Boi!

POPS: Hallelujah Jesus!

CHURCH LADY: The orphanage in my country, Walter?

POPS: Orphanage? Yes?

CHURCH LADY: It suffered horrible flood.

POPS: The orphanage?! Oh no! Not the orphanage.

CHURCH LADY: You help to rebuild it—yes? Oh!

POPS: Oh sure—you mean like—

CHURCH LADY: Money. Much money— Oh!

POPS: Oh hell yeah! Money's no object—you can have it all— oh—I just, am I breathing right? . . . Because this is—oh my—

CHURCH LADY: What?

POPS: This is—this is—

CHURCH LADY: What, Walter?

POPS: This is incredible—but—I really do believe I need an ambulance!

CHURCH LADY: Funny man!

POPS: No. Serious man! Very serious. Call the ambulance! Call Junior. Call Delores. Call— Oh my, you hear that??!!

CHURCH LADY: Hear what?

POPS: You hear that, Delores?

CHURCH LADY: Breathe, Walter—please!

POPS: "Always we are free!"

CHURCH LADY: That's right, Walter—

POPS: Always, yes—always free—this is the greatest—moment of my life.

(Pops collapses.)

CHURCH LADY: Santa, Santa—breathe!

(Blackout.)

SCENE 2

Pops's Bedroom. Midnight. A Week Later.

Pops is very ill. EKG-monitor and IV. A nice bouquet of flowers is by his bedside.

JUNIOR: Hey Pop . . . . Pop?

POPS: . . . Junior?

JUNIOR: Yeah, Pop, it's me—Junior . . . How you feelin', Pop?

POPS: Where you been at, Junior?

JUNIOR: I been here, Pop.

POPS: Here since when?

JUNIOR: You been—you been in a state of unconsciousness, Pop.

POPS: Yeah, I know where *I* been, I'm askin' where have *you* been.

JUNIOR: Can I get you anything, Pop?

POPS: No.

JUNIOR: . . . I see you got the dog nestled in there under them covers with you.

POPS: Fuckin' dog—he's what you call a codependent. Can't shake the motherfucker. He like a bill collector—always up your ass . . . Now: Lulu told you my last wishes?

JUNIOR: Let's just focus on you getting better, Pop.

POPS: Listen to me: no funeral, no wake, no burial, no refreshments, no nothing! Your Uncle Floyd was an undertaker— they're all fuckin' licensed thieves. Don't let them talk you into nothing but ashes and a tin cup.

JUNIOR: The Army or the NYPD gonna cover that if it happens, Pop.

POPS: Don't count on it.

JUNIOR: Police is taking care of your medical right now.

POPS: Since when?

JUNIOR: Lulu said some cop in a suit came to the hospital, they signed for everything, including home-care.

POPS: Well, if a bill come, don't pay it.

JUNIOR: Pop—

POPS: On my bureau is me and your mother's old ATM-card from Chase Manhattan. There should be 'bout 385 dollars in there, withdraw all of it first thing in the morning, cuz when I go, they'll try to hold on to that too.

JUNIOR: Doctor says you could pull through this—

POPS: Yeah, they said the same shit about your mother too. Just do as I say!

JUNIOR: Okay.

POPS: Good. Okay then. I'm tired now, Son.

JUNIOR: Okay . . . I was just . . .

POPS: Whatchu need now?

JUNIOR: I don't need anything, Pop. Just . . . I was hoping we could—talk.

POPS: That ain't what we just did?

JUNIOR: . . . Look, Pop: I just, I wanna tell you—

POPS: Don't start.

JUNIOR: I know I haven't been a very good son to you.

POPS: Stop it!

JUNIOR: Stop what?!

POPS: Just stop it!

JUNIOR: What—I can't say nothing here?! I can't tell you I'm sorry and I'm scared to death and—

POPS: Just stop already!

JUNIOR: I can't tell you I love you, Pop?! I can't tell you—

POPS: You wanna kill me—keep talking!!

JUNIOR: How's me talking gonna kill you?!

POPS: I don't wanna hear it!

JUNIOR: Well maybe I need to say it! Maybe your *son* needs to say it! Maybe your wife needed to say it—or to fuckin' hear it—even once! Just once! You ever fuckin' think of that?!

POPS: Okay. You been heard. But now you gotta stop yelling and take a look around, see who's in the bed and who's up on two feet.

JUNIOR: Why? What's the difference? I could be the one in the bed, and it'd be the exact same cold fuckin' shit with you. Ask Mom. Yeah. She made excuses for you all her life. But she lived it. She fuckin', she was, she . . .

(Beat.)

. . . Oh man. Aw man. I'm sorry, Pop.

POPS: Stop it.

JUNIOR: Oh man.

POPS: Hey, hey. Go get me some water, would ya?

JUNIOR: . . . Yeah . . . Yeah, sure. You want it cold? Warm? With ice? How you want it, Pop?

POPS: Just from the tap.

JUNIOR: Okay.

POPS: Yeah. People look down their nose at tap water. Makes me wanna slap a motherfucker. Tap water is good water. Don't ever forget that, Son.

JUNIOR: I won't, Pop.

POPS: It's damn good water.

JUNIOR: It is.

POPS: And another thing: eat vegetables. Partake of a fiber-rich diet.

JUNIOR: I will.

POPS: Fiber's your best friend, Son.

JUNIOR: Okay, Pop.

POPS: Potassium combats high blood pressure. A black man needs that.

JUNIOR: Yes he does.

POPS: Okay then. Glad we spoke on that.

JUNIOR: . . . Me too, Pop.

(Junior goes to get the water, then turns and stares at Pops.)

POPS: . . . . What?

JUNIOR: Nothing, just . . . You still gonna be here when I get back—right?

POPS: Where the fuck else I'm gonna be?

JUNIOR: . . . Never mind . . . Sorry . . .

POPS: You weak, Son, you know that? . . . Siddown.

JUNIOR: I'll just go get you the water.

POPS: Sit down . . . . . . Now I ain't a talker—

JUNIOR: Yeah, and that's okay, Pop, cuz I—

POPS: Hey, you wanna hear me say something or not?

JUNIOR: I do, but I just wanna let ya know—

POPS: Boy, you just like your mama, always wanna be interjecting shit.

JUNIOR: . . . Moms did always have something to say, didn't she?

POPS: Oh boy . . . . On our wedding night, she was nervous, right there in the bed there she was in her negligee chatting away about this and that and every little damn thing crossed her mind till finally the sun started coming up through the window and I told her: "Delores you sure do got a way with words—but there are other forms of communication."

JUNIOR: She told me that story. Said you were a real gentleman.

POPS: Did she tell ya it took me ten nights before she let me proceed with the intimacies?

JUNIOR: She told me that too.

POPS: Yeah, I bet she told you a whole lotta bad shit about me too—her little confidant.

JUNIOR: Marriage got bumps.

POPS: I never told you about my father—

JUNIOR: Mom did.

POPS: Well shit, is there anything your mama didn't tell you? If you already know everything, why can't I just go to sleep?

JUNIOR: Tell me 'bout your daddy, Pops.

POPS: But you already know!

JUNIOR: Just tell me.

POPS: Why? I didn't never know him, he was a traveling man, I hated him.

JUNIOR: Okay. And then what?

POPS: That's it. I hated him. And I lived my own life in reaction to that.

JUNIOR: How'd ya do that?

POPS: You know, everything the opposite. Married your mother. Joined the police. Paid taxes. Bought insurance. Got a Riverside Drive apartment. Had you. Put down firm roots. Be a fucking man.

JUNIOR: And you did that, Pop. And what I said before—

POPS: Mo Lubenthal came to see me after I'd been shot, I told him: "How much can we get, Mo"? He told me: "I was drunk and where I wasn't supposed to be and they could toss me a few pennies or just fire me if I pushed it too far—unless I maybe told them the boy called me nigger." —So I went with that.

JUNIOR: So what? That don't change nothing.

POPS: The point is: the day I got shot? I think I was relieved. Because I could stop pretending to be some guy I wasn't never meant to be. Trying to live in reaction to my father turned me angry, drunk and half outta my mind. Don't do the same like me, Son. It ain't necessary. Because in reality, I'm more like my daddy than I thought. And I only learned it the night of my little heart attack last Sunday. And if I survive this, I just might take to the road and travel a little myself—do a little wandering.

JUNIOR: Wandering where?

POPS: Now tell me 'bout Lulu—pregnant or not?

JUNIOR: Not.

POPS: And that's good news or bad?

JUNIOR: Good.

POPS: Okay, but just cuz you didn't break it—don't mean you ain't bought it, right?

JUNIOR: Meaning what?

POPS: Meaning, move on—but she deserves a soft landing-spot for herself before she move on from here. Now: you go on and keep an eye on them movers—make sure they don't steal nothing.

JUNIOR: City called off the movers.

POPS: When?

JUNIOR: 'Bout a day after you was taken to the hospital according to Lulu.

POPS: And what about Audrey and Dave—they come by again?

JUNIOR: They came again the last two days, but Lulu had the doctor tell them you couldn't be disturbed.

POPS: Is that so?

JUNIOR: That's what she told me.

POPS: Hmmm . . . Call Mo Lubenthal in the morning, tell 'em I'm ready to deal.

JUNIOR: I don't think there's a deal to be made now—

POPS: Just do it.

JUNIOR: Okay, Pop.

POPS: Good. Now—it's okay with you I get a little fuckin' post–heart attack rest? And hey—take these goddamn awful-smelling flowers outta here—who wasted their money on them anyway?

JUNIOR: I did, Pop.

POPS: Fine. Leave 'em then. Now if I tell you I love you, will you let me sleep?

JUNIOR: I love you, Pop.

POPS: Same to you. Alright? Good night, God bless—take the goddamn dog, and get the fuck out.

(Blackout.)

SCENE 3

The Apartment. Evening. Two Days Later.

The stage opens itself in such a way that all of the following is simultaneously visible:

Pops is in his bedroom. An EKG-monitor, an IV, and an adjustable food tray are by his bed. A male nurse (the actor playing Oswaldo) tends to him. Detective O'Connor sits in a chair by his side. Pops stares up at the ceiling. Detective O'Connor stares at Pops.

Just outside the bedroom, Lulu sits on one of several folding chairs outside the bedroom. She's reading a magazine, keeping vigil, and ready to enter the bedroom if she's called on.

Just inside the apartment's front door stands Junior. On the other side of the door is the Church Lady. Midstream:

JUNIOR: —What I'm saying is you ain't welcome here.

CHURCH LADY: I'm here to see your father.

JUNIOR: I've asked you twice nicely to go wait in the lobby.

CHURCH LADY: I have a right to see Walter.

JUNIOR: Look: I know women who would break a bitch like you in two for a dime bag and a Happy Meal, okay? Now: you ain't gettin' my father's money, neither is your church, I'll hurt you if I have to, so stay the fuck away.

(Lieutenant Caro approaches the front door.)

LIEUTENANT CARO: Problem here?
JUNIOR: Oh, no—not at all.

(Lieutenant Caro extends his hand to the Church Lady.)

LIEUTENANT CARO: Dave Caro, how you doin'?
CHURCH LADY: I know you!
LIEUTENANT CARO: Could be . . . Junior—Dave Caro, from dinner a couple weeks ago?
JUNIOR: Oh yeah. Hey man.
LIEUTENANT CARO: Audrey's in with your father—mind if I?
JUNIOR: Right down the hall.
LIEUTENANT CARO: Take my card. For anything. We're practically family now.

(Lieutenant Caro hands Junior a card, and enters the apartment.)

JUNIOR *(To the Church Lady)*: Stay away from my father!

(Junior closes the door on the Church Lady and locks it. Lieutenant Caro approaches Lulu.)

LIEUTENANT CARO: Dave Caro, you're Junior's fiancée?
LULU: Girlfriend. But I mean, we're discussing future plans, but—
LIEUTENANT CARO: How's Walter doing?
LULU: So so.
LIEUTENANT CARO: What's his prognosis?
LULU: Oh, it's pneumonia now, not prognosis.
LIEUTENANT CARO: I see.

(Lieutenant Caro enters the bedroom.
Junior hands Lulu a beer sits down next to her, as:)

DETECTIVE O'CONNOR: Eat the pound cake. I know you like pound cake, Walter.

POPS: Don't like the kind with the stripes—you oughta know that.

LIEUTENANT CARO: I gotta say, Walter, full medical care in your own apartment, courtesy of the NYPD? I mean—Donald Trump—maybe—*maybe* Trump gets full medical care from the convenience of his home—

POPS: Ain't gonna be my home much longer, now is it?

LIEUTENANT CARO: Actually, that's why we're here.

POPS: A week ago, y'all had me evicted, warrants out on my son, bank account froze, shit confiscated—

LIEUTENANT CARO: The city, Walter, is ready to turn the page.

DETECTIVE O'CONNOR: It's useless, Dave. Walter seems determined to go down in flames—

POPS: I hope I die tonight! I hope it come on NY1 bright and early tomorrow morning: how the city harassed, threatened, strong-armed, and put out on the street a feeble old patriotic, tax-paying, African-American ex-cop war hero senior citizen—and how they didn't stop the barrage till he dropped dead as a doornail.

LIEUTENANT CARO: You're overestimating your position here.

DETECTIVE O'CONNOR: Dave's right. I wouldn't lie to you.

LIEUTENANT CARO: Eight years ago, you overplayed your hand. That's the reason you're in the spot you're in today. However, I spoke to your lawyer, Mr. Liebenthal—

POPS: Lubenthal—

LIEUTENANT CARO: Exactly, yes. Your lawyer Lubenthal is ready to sign off on our confidentiality agreement and the concessions to you that come with it.

POPS: How much money?

LIEUTENANT CARO: Unfortunately: no money. Once you turned down that final offer, money came off the table. Money implies liability—and once you turned down the final settlement offer—

POPS: So what I get?

LIEUTENANT CARO: You get your apartment back plus eighteen months free rent. The city agrees to expunge your son's entire criminal record—now that's subject to him avoiding arrest for the next fifteen years—but to employers and creditors, it'll be like he never even had a parking ticket. And obviously, all the dust that's been kicked up the last couple of weeks—that will all disappear entirely. And the city will cover your remaining legal fees, but Mr. Liebental tells us he hasn't cashed a check of yours in over a year anyway, and he's not interested in payment past, present, or future, only that your well-being be secured legally and in writing. Finally—as a conciliatory gesture, you'll be invited annually and be made a member of the advisory boards of the mayor's annual galas for both "Jack and Jill of America, Incorporated" and the AAMA.

POPS: And that's what?

LIEUTENANT CARO: The African-American Museum Association I believe. Yes. And both those organizations, when you're on the board, you get on the list for free tickets to a variety of cultural and sporting events.

POPS: But no money.

LIEUTENANT CARO: I wish there was, but no. If you hadn't turned down that final settlement offer—

POPS: Look, I'll admit I want this to be over. But: no money, no signature on the nondisclosure. I'm old, I'm gonna die soon anyway, so any discomfort I can cause you people, unless there's some money involved . . .

LIEUTENANT CARO: There is a discretionary fund—

POPS: Aha!! How much?

LIEUTENANT CARO: Fifteen grand.

POPS: Fifteen grand—that comes to what? Twenty-five hundred per bullet inside me?

DETECTIVE O'CONNOR: Please take it, Walter—you'll have your pension, social security—you can have your life back—and you can help Junior with his. I know you want that.

POPS: Fifteen grand?

LIEUTENANT CARO: Fifteen. Cashier's check. Untaxed. Like you found it in the street. Plus everything else in the package.

POPS: I'll take forty.

LIEUTENANT CARO: Fifteen.

POPS: Thirty.

LIEUTENANT CARO: Fifteen.

POPS: I'll sign it right now, but for twenty grand, okay?

LIEUTENANT CARO: The number is fifteen, Walter, and if you try for a penny more, that's just gonna kick in their "Fuck It Factor."

POPS: What's that?

LIEUTENANT CARO: It's the point in a negotiation, Walter, where the powers that be revise the cost benefit, reassess the risk, and end up saying: "You know what? Paying this guy ain't worth it, let's just crush him—Fuck It."

DETECTIVE O'CONNOR: Don't do this to yourself. And don't do this to Junior.

LIEUTENANT CARO: Don't do this to Audrey—she loves you. Or to Junior. You were wronged, Walter. But destroying yourself and your loved ones won't right that wrong. It's been eight years. Let it go, man. In my heart, Walter, I know you want to put this burden down. It's okay. Let it go.

POPS: . . . . . . Oh man.

LIEUTENANT CARO: You know I'm right.

POPS: . . . What should I do here, Audrey?

DETECTIVE O'CONNOR: I just want you to walk me down that aisle, Walter. I just want to put all of this behind us—I don't even know how things went so far afield. Junior deserves a second chance. And you deserve to keep your apartment and everything you've worked so hard for. You're like my father. And Dave has grown so fond of you—he so respects your guts and your principles and he really just wants to take you fishing out on the Island—

LIEUTENANT CARO: I mean, I don't wanna force myself on you, Walter. Or this deal either for that matter. It has to be what you want to do.

POPS: But, Dave—it would be a help to you, if I signed the nondisclosure?

LIEUTENANT CARO: Very helpful, Walter, I won't lie.

POPS: Almost like a wedding present?

LIEUTENANT CARO: It'd be one hell of a wedding present, yeah. But again—only if it's what you want.

POPS: Audrey?

DETECTIVE O'CONNOR: Only if you feel it's right for you. But, yes. Do it.

POPS: Okay then.

DETECTIVE O'CONNOR: Oh God, thank you, Walter!

POPS: Get me a pen—I'll sign.

DETECTIVE O'CONNOR: Thank you!

LIEUTENANT CARO: Oh my God—you're the man, Walter— you're a goddamn rock star is what you are! You're friggin' Jimi Hendrix at Monterey!

POPS: Fifteen grand. And I'll take the ring.

LIEUTENANT CARO: The ring? What ring?

DETECTIVE O'CONNOR: My engagement ring?

POPS: That'd be the one, yep. Fifteen grand and the ring, we can call the whole thing even—whaddya say?

LIEUTENANT CARO: What?! The ring?! You're joking, right?!

DETECTIVE O'CONNOR: You want my ring?

LIEUTENANT CARO: Hey, hey—fuck that—this is a joke, right? Because if not—I mean, no offense, but go fuck yourself man!

POPS: Now that ain't a nice way to talk, Dave.

LIEUTENANT CARO: Okay, but this is a joke, right? Cuz, Walter, you're making me a little fuckin' nervous over here—

DETECTIVE O'CONNOR: You're not serious, are you, Walter?

LIEUTENANT CARO: Of course he's not serious! Now Walter, here's a pen, and here's the thing—

DETECTIVE O'CONNOR: I think he's serious, Dave.

LIEUTENANT CARO: Okay, Walter—Audrey's starting to get upset.

POPS: I'm sorry to hear that. But you do need my signature, doncha, Dave?

LIEUTENANT CARO: I don't need anything!

DETECTIVE O'CONNOR: Why do you want my ring, Walter?!

LIEUTENANT CARO: Hey! Everybody slow down! This settlement, believe me, this is a gift we're handing you, Walter!

POPS: And I'll always cherish it—along with the ring.

LIEUTENANT CARO: "Along with the ring"?! Along with what ring, Walter—cuz you're not ever getting her fuckin' ring— so straighten up and fly fuckin' right over here before you get hurt!

(Junior and Lulu enter the bedroom.)

JUNIOR: Everything okay in here?

POPS: Everything is fine, just finalizing some negotiations is all.

LIEUTENANT CARO: Oh I'm telling you right now: there are no negotiations being finalized right now!

JUNIOR *(To Lieutenant Caro)*: Look man—maybe you should leave.

LIEUTENANT CARO: Excuse me? I should leave? Excuse me?

POPS: Hey hey, leave us be, Junior. This will all be over shortly.

JUNIOR: You sure, Pop?

DETECTIVE O'CONNOR: It's okay, Junior.

JUNIOR: Okay then.

(Junior and Lulu exit. Beat.)

LIEUTENANT CARO: Walter.

POPS: Dave.

LIEUTENANT CARO: Wow. I am disappointed in you, Walter.

POPS: I imagine you would be.

LIEUTENANT CARO: I mean. I didn't wanna have to go here, but I think this is the moment where I need to tell you just a few things about Dave Caro—

POPS: Before you get to that: your father—he didn't never eat his gun, did he?

LIEUTENANT CARO: My father's a retired electrician living in Fort Myers. I'm just here to do a job, Walter—whaddya want from me?

POPS: I thought so. You good though. Okay then. I'll take the fifteen grand cashier's check, the ring—and what I want from you, Dave—is your necktie.

LIEUTENANT CARO: My necktie?! What are we—kids in a school yard?! What the fuck is wrong with you?!

DETECTIVE O'CONNOR: You really want the ring, Walter? My ring?

LIEUTENANT CARO: Audrey, this man is so far beneath you, he's under the ground halfway to China!

DETECTIVE O'CONNOR: Why do you want my ring, Walter?

LIEUTENANT CARO: Okay, enough. There is a line, Walter. A line of demarcation from which, once you cross it, you can never go back. You are perilously close to crossing that line.

POPS: Look Dave: The Ring. The Check. The Necktie—or go fuck yourself.

LIEUTENANT CARO: I'll arrest Junior right now, Walter—toss his ass in a cell with gangbangers and make sure the system loses him for two weeks minimum—and that's just the tip of the iceberg of what I can and will do to him—right this very minute—if you don't come quickly to your senses over here. Now is that what you want?

DETECTIVE O'CONNOR: Dave—why don't you leave the room and let me talk with Walter?

LIEUTENANT CARO: Audrey, I love you, but please—let me handle this.

POPS: Handle what? You wanna arrest Junior? Go ahead. Arrest him.

DETECTIVE O'CONNOR: Nobody's going to arrest Junior!

LIEUTENANT CARO: Audrey—stay out of this!

DETECTIVE O'CONNOR: Why do you want my ring, Walter?

LIEUTENANT CARO: If you don't care about your son, Walter— then at least look out for yourself! You're an old bitter drunk—

DETECTIVE O'CONNOR: Dave!

LIEUTENANT CARO: And maybe you don't think things can't get worse—but believe me, they fuckin' can—and they will! You don't like me? Hey fuck you, I don't like you either— but who the fuck am I? I'm just a cog in the wheel, Walter—and so are you! And the wheel's gonna keep turning whether it's gotta grind out your guts or not—either way, the wheel don't feel a fuckin' thing! The wheel don't give a fuck, Walter. And you know that! But somewhere inside that thick head of yours—I know you give a fuck! I know you do! And I know you're reasonable! You think by saying: "Fuck you" that you're showing the world that you got balls—but Walter, unless I'm mistaken—no disrespect— but that fuckin' rookie cop shot off your balls eight years ago—so what's the fuckin' point, here?!

DETECTIVE O'CONNOR: Walter, please—

POPS: Audrey, Dave: I'm going to the bathroom now to make a deposit—while I'm gone, y'all can sort it out if you want my signature—or if you wanna explain to your bosses, Dave, how you fucked this shit all up, okay? You can have a victory—or you can have a ring. Can't have both. *(Shouts)* Lulu, I need an escort to the office!!! . . .

DETECTIVE O'CONNOR: Why do you want my ring, Walter?!

POPS: Because it pleases me to take it from you—okay?

DETECTIVE O'CONNOR: That's not an answer, Walter.

POPS: Then I'll leave it to you to provide yourself one.

(Lulu enters.)

LULU: I'm here, Dad.

LIEUTENANT CARO: This is nonsense, Walter—It's not our fault you got shot, it's not our fault you got stupid and greedy, it's not our fault you're a lying, shiftless drunk—and I'll bet my life that kid never called you a fuckin' nigger in the first place!

POPS: And Dave—hey—you may very well be right. So now: The Ring. The Cashier's Check. The Necktie. Or—go fuck yourself. Do you want this over or not?

LIEUTENANT CARO: Walter, I'm begging you to reconsider—

POPS: Looky here—I ain't quick in the bathroom, so you'll have time to mull it over . . . Hey: toughen up now, Audrey, I taught you better than that.

DETECTIVE O'CONNOR: But this isn't right. It isn't right, Walter.

POPS: What exactly isn't right, Audrey? And what a world it would be if "what was right" was enough. Besides—nothing's been decided here.

LIEUTENANT CARO: Oh, you know goddamn well it has!

POPS: I don't know nothin' 'bout nothin' and I'm fine either way. Your call, Dave. Do you want this win or not?

LIEUTENANT CARO: This is bullshit.

POPS: Nah, Kemosabe, this is poker—and see, I play a little too.

(Lulu helps Pops walk out the door. As they exit:)

DETECTIVE O'CONNOR: But this isn't right!

POPS: You be well, Audrey.

SCENE 4

The Kitchen. The Roof.

Six months later. Winter. The kitchen. Junior now sits in his father's place in the wheelchair at the kitchen table. He sips a from a twenty-ounce can of beer and is reading the paper. He is dressed in winter clothes.

After a moment, Oswaldo enters, wearing a cheap winter parka over a cheap suit. He is wheeling a carry-on luggage-type bag behind him.

JUNIOR: Job interview?

OSWALDO: Yeah.

JUNIOR: How'd it go?

OSWALDO: I think it went positive. More or less.

JUNIOR: Good.

OSWALDO: But maybe more "less" than "more."

JUNIOR: Tough out there.

OSWALDO: Word.

(Oswaldo goes into his bag and pulls out Ring Dings, bologna, and Fanta Grape. He sits at the table with Junior.)

You want a Ring Ding?

JUNIOR: Okay.

OSWALDO: Bologna or plain?

JUNIOR: Plain.

OSWALDO: Here ya go . . . And yo, I just wanna say again—
I really appreciate you letting me stay here again.

JUNIOR: It ain't a thing.

OSWALDO: I appreciate it though.

(Lulu enters. She is not pregnant.)

LULU: Morning, Junior.

JUNIOR: Morning, Lulu.

LULU: Morning, Oswaldo.

OSWALDO: Ring Ding?

LULU: Sure.

OSWALDO: Bologna or plain?

LULU: Bologna.

STEPHEN ADLY GUIRGIS

(She goes to the fridge, retrieves a soda. Beat.)

Did Dad call?

JUNIOR: You ask me that every day, Lulu.

LULU: Oh. I just thought maybe he called.

JUNIOR: Nope.

LULU: . . . So, um—how's school, Junior?

JUNIOR: Good.

LULU: That's good . . . . . . My school's good too.

JUNIOR: Good.

LULU: So, do you think he'll be home for Christmas though?

JUNIOR: Who?

LULU: Dad.

JUNIOR: Who knows? The man went up to the roof in a fedora
and a suit with the dog—that was four months ago.

LULU: Feels longer.

JUNIOR: Is what it is . . .

(Junior takes a long swig of beer.)

Oswaldo—I could get another Ring Ding?

·   ·   ·

(Two weeks after Pops's last scene. On the roof. Summer.
Walter is dressed in a suit and is wearing Dave's distinctive
tie. He carries his cane. At his feet is a traveling bag and a small
pet carrier. Next to him is the Church Lady.)

POPS: I'm glad you agreed to see me.

CHURCH LADY: I thought I had killed you that night.

POPS: But you didn't.

CHURCH LADY: Thanks, God. You taking a trip?

POPS: I am.

CHURCH LADY: And who is in that pet cage?

POPS: Who you think?

CHURCH LADY: "That Little Motherfucker."

POPS: That's right.

CHURCH LADY: What happened between us, Walter—please— I hope you are not asking me to travel with you, like romance—

POPS: Oh no, no.

CHURCH LADY: It was not so good what happened that night.

POPS: Whatever the hell happened that night, it got me to here. And I didn't do nothing to deserve it. You gave that to me. You gave me grace. "Always be free," right?

CHURCH LADY: Yes.

POPS: See, I just wanted to give you something 'fore I left. Here.

(Pops hands her the diamond ring.)

CHURCH LADY: Walter—I cannot.

POPS: No no, I'm not proposing marriage to you. I'm giving it to you. For them lepers you was talking about.

CHURCH LADY: Orphans, Walter—not lepers.

POPS: Even better. For the orphans then.

CHURCH LADY: This ring—it is too valuable.

POPS: Retails for 30K—it's valuable alright. But you more valuable. To me. Do something good with it. For them orphans down there.

CHURCH LADY: Walter—

POPS: I ain't asking. So you ought to respect your elders and just take it.

CHURCH LADY: I can't take it.

POPS: Why not?

CHURCH LADY: Glenda, the church lady, she told me about you. I clean the church, and she was always there. Lonely. So she talk to me. She told me everything about you.

POPS: So?

CHURCH LADY: So I tell her the priest want her to visit someone else. I came in her place. Because I know all about you. From Glenda. I came to rob you. To tell you stories and make you give me what you have. That's what I do. That's who I am.

POPS: That's not all you are. You changed me.

CHURCH LADY: You changed yourself.

POPS: So, you change yourself then. Keep the ring.

CHURCH LADY: What about your son?

POPS: I took care of him. He'll be fine. Or he won't.

CHURCH LADY: But Walter.

POPS: What is it?

CHURCH LADY: Don't you understand? There are no orphans, Walter. Do you understand me? There are no orphans.

(Walter gives her the ring, kisses her cheek.)

POPS: Well—there are orphans somewhere.

(Walter exits to the staircase with his travel bag and pet carrier.
The Church Lady remains alone.
She stares out at the horizon.
The lights fade.)

END OF PLAY